LET'S TALK ABOUT

LET'S TALK ABOUT

Fifth

Teaching Ballet in the 21ˢᵗ Century

DEBORAH ENGERMAN

TANTSI PUBLISHING

Let's Talk About Fifth: Teaching Ballet in the Twenty-First Century

Copyright © 2023 by Tantsi Publishing

Published by Tantsi Publishing

Cover Design and Interior Book Design by Susi Clark, Creative Blueprint Design
Front Cover Photo by Scott Serio
Dancer on Cover: Magnolia Williams
Back Cover Photo by Ashley Smith, Wide-Eyed Studios
Interior Photos by Scott Serio and Ashley Smith, Wide-Eyed Studios
Proofreading by Ellen Polk, EllenEdits
Indexing by Birgitte Necessary

Dancers in Interior Photos: Adrienne Canterna, Kelly Sneddon, Christine Blackshaw, Natalie Fitch, Jada Simms, Rilee Anderson, Madison Zinkand, Liz Devanney, Emily Bailey, Magnolia Williams, Bella Brown, Ava Horodowicz, Gianna Amand, Jasmine Simms, and Julia Beyers

ISBN Paperback: 979-8-218-23793-6

Contents

"Deborah Engerman is one of the reasons classical ballet is the love of my life! She taught me passion, patience, attention to detail, selflessness, vulnerability, drama, perseverance, courage, determination, and respect—respect for the art and for myself. Respect for the past, present, and future of ballet. She was my mirror in the most wonderful way. I'm so grateful to have learned from her and many other uniquely talented and brilliant human beings. I'm grateful every day I had such incredible training."

Adrienne Canterna

"The information I learned from Deborah Engerman was paramount to saving my knees and hips. I learned that I don't have to be the ideal size or shape for ballet to pursue the art form. Passion and a healthy dose of dedication."

Maddie Burnham

"The most influential ballet teacher I have had is Mrs. Deborah Engerman. My outlook on ballet completely changed when I began working with her. I believe it was meant to be that I fell into Mrs. Deborah's lap at the age I did. It was in those important years that my talent could have remained the same or could have been formed into a talent I could have a profession with. Without having Mrs. Deborah as my teacher, I very well may not have gone to a university for dance, let alone pursued a career in it.

Mrs. Deborah gave me my technical foundation and I could not be more thankful for that. A student can have many teachers in their lifetime, but there is usually one teacher a student can always look at as their turning point. Mrs. Deborah taught me many things about technique and life. She had many different approaches to help students; some she used on me and some I saw her use with other students. Every student learns differently, and Mrs. Deborah was always very good about changing her teaching approaches based on the student and how they learned best."

Kerry Bruso

I don't recall a distinct moment when I fell in love with dancing or, specifically, with ballet. I simply never defined myself as anything other than a dancer. Dance was and still is the love that found me. Today, as an adult, I can intellectualize my connection to dance. I can say it represents the best of who we are as humans, toiling together, through movement, in the ceaseless pursuit of beauty, meaning, and the ideal. We know we will never achieve perfection—we don't even care. The search, the mental, emotional, and physical aspirations are, in and of themselves, what drives us. The internal and external striving of our minds, bodies, and hearts—the sensation of this venture is the destination, as much as the ideal arabesque could ever be. Ballet grows bigger and deeper for me, unfolding itself endlessly, the more I know of it. All of this is my truth. All these fancy thoughts. And yet, in the end, I love it because I simply do.

I also adore teaching ballet and have dedicated countless hours to scouring books, videos, and any other content about dancing and instruction I can get my hands on. I imagine I'm not the only one. Through my years of teaching and reading, I have learned there is a space between the lettered pedagogy of ballet and what it takes to infuse its knowledge into students to help them develop as dancers. I desire to fill that gap by offering this book to other ballet lovers and teachers at any stage of their careers. In more than twenty-five years as a teacher, I have trained students from the recreational dancer to those who have gone on to professional careers to some who have become successful ballet teachers themselves. I know what good teaching is because I have lived it.

So how did I begin?

My mother signed me up for a ballet class when I was young—I hadn't asked for it. She had recently taken my younger sister to the pediatrician, concerned because my sister was not sprawling about for hours in a split in her crib the way I had done years before. The doctor assured my mother that my sister was healthy, that I was the unusual one, and that I would presumably be good at ballet or gymnastics. My mom followed the doctor's advice, and that's how, at age five, I landed in a ballet class.

I started at Harriet Eisner's recreational dance studio in Baltimore, Maryland, where I was promoted onto pointe at age nine—way too early. Nonetheless, it was Miss Harriet who provided my young heart with the space and guidance to fall in love with ballet. I can vividly remember the first time in her class that I heard the music to "Waltz of the Flowers" from *The Nutcracker*, as we were learning a dance to it. I believe my heart exploded all over the dance studio that day, and it's never been put together the same way again. I am grateful for her encouragement and loving introduction to the art that will always be my guiding light. At the age of ten, I wanted better training and transitioned to the Wally Saunders Dance Studio in Pikesville, Maryland, where Mr. Saunders promptly took me off pointe for a full year. A more knowledgeable director and teacher, he recognized that putting a student on pointe at nine years old was a misguided decision, regardless of potential. Working on pointe that young can damage the healthy development of the foot and toes. Although at the time I was devastated, I later came to understand and wholeheartedly agree with his position. Sufficient training and physical development are crucial to ensuring the safety of dancers before they begin pointe work.

After a few years, Mr. Saunders suggested I move to a ballet school attached to a professional performing company with a history of producing professional dancers. I thus began studying with the Baltimore Ballet School, originally the Maryland Ballet School. There, under the direction of Wendy Robinson, I attended daily ballet classes and took some of the Royal Academy of Dance (RAD) graded exams. I also spent a couple of summers studying at the National Academy of the Arts (later to become the Virginia School of the Arts), under the direction of Petrus Bosman. Throughout these teenage training years, I had the opportunity to perform with the Baltimore Ballet School, National Academy of the Arts, and another Baltimore school and performing company, the Cultural Arts Center. The ballets I danced in included *The Nutcracker* (in which I performed the roles of Clara and the Sugar Plum Fairy), *La Bayadère, Paquita*, and *The Magical Music Box* (in which I danced as the Muse).

A strain to my left calf during my senior year of high school interrupted my training for a few months. This injury also coincided with college application season. I was attending a private, independent college prep school and had grown up in a culture where pursuing dance professionally was discouraged. I'd had to persuade my parents and my school to allow me to take ballet classes instead of pursuing sports. Although I longed to dance and knew that some people became professional dancers and artists, I was raised to pursue a practical, academic career. The adults around me had such careers—my mother a teacher, my father an attorney, my best friend's parents both doctors. I believed, in my naïveté, that these sorts of jobs held my only real-life options. I got the message: a dance career was not a good choice.

Thus, I found myself at Dickinson College, majoring in International Policy and Management Studies. But I couldn't leave ballet behind. Dickinson College is in Carlisle, Pennsylvania, also home to Central Pennsylvania Youth Ballet (CPYB). So, while I toiled at Dickinson in classes like "Policy Writing and Implementation," "Polimetrics," and "World Religions," I was also taking dance classes with the faculty of CPYB and performing regularly with our college dance company, the Dance Theatre Group, under the direction of Christine Vilardo. There, I was introduced to an eclectic mix of dance styles. I learned modern, lyrical, and contemporary dance, and performed in Ms. Vilardo's premiering pieces, which included "Terra Firma" and "Holding Patterns."

After graduation, I quit dancing again, believing I was making the grown-up decision to lead a "serious" life as an attorney or a diplomat. I still bought into the idea that an educated woman would never choose to be an artist—that dance could never be a career. I don't recall feeling sad at the time; I simply suppressed my love and attachment to ballet. But what I came to learn later was that I had closed myself off from the depths of my heart, where ballet lives.

A year after college graduation, one of my closest high school friends died from suicide. A life-altering tragedy. For a few months, I lost my way. Besides the grief and guilt I felt over the loss of my friend, I experienced existential pain. I didn't know who I was or what my place in the world was supposed to be. I questioned why I was even alive, why I was put here on earth. The shock and trauma of losing my friend in such a horrific manner prompted a deluge of feelings about the life I'd left behind— my life in dance.

Simultaneously, I was, for the first time in my life, realizing I was not immortal. I felt panic about how I was going to spend the time I had and what I would make of it. I admitted to myself that without dance, my life felt empty. And this was no way to live. Eventually, I accepted that I didn't have to define my life as dictated by the culture around me. It was within my power, and was therefore my responsibility, to pursue a life doing something I loved, with a clear sense of purpose.

So, at age twenty-three, I left my corporate job and went back to school at Towson University in Maryland. I followed the Towson University dance education curriculum without fully matriculating for another degree, taking all the dance and dance education courses I needed to attend graduate school. My course requirements included assistant teaching at Towson's Children's Dance Division, a dance academy at Towson University for primary and secondary school students. There in the classroom, I found my calling: teaching students ages nine through their early twenties, the time during which professional dancers receive their career training. No graduate degree required.

In the ballet classroom, I was home. I felt confident because I was successful in bringing my knowledge to these artists in training. I was happy because I felt purposeful and was sharing one of the true loves in my life. And that's what I've been doing ever since.

I undertook my first paid job in the ballet world as teaching assistant to Mary Schaefer, both at Towson University's Children's Division and at the Kingsville Recreation Center in Kingsville, Maryland. From there, my career advanced. I went on to teach, coach, and choreograph at multiple schools in Maryland and Pennsylvania. I have never lost interest in ballet or in the students I teach. My journey has brought me to wonderful schools and second-rate schools. I have worked for the full spectrum: knowledgeable directors who relied on me to maintain their high standards and less-schooled directors who leaned on me to bring solid ballet instruction to their academies, directors who were ethical and others who were dishonest, directors who ran their business well and a few who were disorganized. Throughout all of it, my passion remained the same: teach these humans to dance! Specifically, teach them ballet.

Now I want to share what I have learned along the way. This book is a compendium of knowledge I've gained over the years, offering real-world, human methods to motivate, teach, and lead today's students in the classical classroom. I write to guide teachers in how to take the technical details of ballet and communicate them in meaningful, effective ways to their students. I include specific descriptions of the classical vocabulary, but my aim is not to provide a sweeping book of ballet vocabulary and technique. I include technical instruction, but I proceed beyond dry descriptions of proper technique by presenting clear-cut, workable ideas about molding the dancers of the future. The photos that accompany the text function as an aid to illustrate the movement and represent dancers at different stages in their training, from an intermediate ballet level through professional performers. I have chosen to show you dancers with a variety of body types and in different phases of their dance careers, because all ballet students deserve excellent teaching.

This guide serves to provide valuable and applicable tools for today's teachers and dancers that fill in the gaps between pedagogy, protocol, and tradition. My driving ambition is that *Let's Talk About Fifth: Teaching Ballet in the Twenty-First Century* will inspire and embolden other teachers and dancers on their own journeys.

Chapter 1

The Ballet Classroom: Teaching Philosophies

Who are we ballet teachers? We love an art form that has been around for hundreds of years, but few people living today have seen a live performance. We obsess over feet, hip rotation, fingers, and the beauty of an unfolding arm. We would recognize anywhere the sound of pointe shoes hitting the floor as dancers travel through space. We strive to conserve an incomparable art and send new dancers into the future to keep it alive and well.

Teaching ballet is not the same as performing ballet. Not even close. There are seasoned, renowned ballerinas in the world who make terrible teachers. And there are fabulous ballet teachers who would never be accepted into a professional ballet company. Each profession demands its own abilities and expertise. And while some people will excel in both areas, it's incorrect to assume someone has talent in both.

Ballet teachers, the good ones, have trained at professional ballet schools or, at least, dance schools with excellent ballet training. The difference between the two types of schools being that a professional ballet school exists exclusively to train ballet dancers. Its classes and performances are primarily ballet based. The professional ballet school is often affiliated with a professional ballet performing company. There are also "all-around" dance schools that offer all styles of training and performances. A handful of these all-around schools offer a professional level of classical ballet training, which its students can bring into the professional ballet world. Ballet teachers from these schools have spent time living the ballet life and have learned the technical aspects of ballet. Teachers should also have had some performing experience to lend wisdom about stage work and artistry. But excellent ballet teachers need not have had full careers with professional companies.

Ballet teachers need the cognitive ability to understand the logistics of classical technique and to be able to break that technique down into steps students can follow. And then there's communication: ballet teachers must communicate clearly what they expect and what ballet expects. It is not enough to simply demonstrate steps and expect every student to be able to execute the movement correctly. That would be an imitation of your example as opposed to an understanding of what they're doing. A demonstrator merely shows movement; a teacher shows (or has a demonstrator show) the movement and, more vitally, *explains* how to perform the movement.

Teaching ballet today is different from the practice a hundred, fifty, even twenty years ago. A host of developments and changes have transformed certain aspects of the teaching environment, the ballet student, and even the ballet teacher. We have all kinds of new technology for playing, recording, and editing music. Cell phones have become omnipresent and have reoriented the entire way we live our twenty-first-century lives. Indeed, this occurs even in the ballet classroom, as students desire to have their phones with them in class (something I do not allow), or at least want to check their phones for text messages at every break. Social media has become a powerful force in how students of today value themselves: specifically, they want more likes, more followers, and fame.

In that vein, the flash moment of a high extension or multiple turns (leading to unsound practices like overstretching and turning on a poorly aligned, weak leg), which show up quickly and easily on social media, are coveted. Today's students rarely enter their training with a yearning for and an understanding of the slow, meticulous training required to build long-lasting, successful careers. In addition, there has been a considerable relaxation of the boundaries between authority figures and students in our culture. This can show up in the ballet classroom as students attempting not to wear the required dress code of a school or finding other ways of breaking whichever rules are in place. And there has been a shift in education from an enterprise in which teachers are respected for their knowledge, trusted to make the best decisions concerning how to teach the subject matter, and expected to make the demand of effort from their students to a more transactional endeavor, where the student is "owed" something as a paying customer. This paradigm shift shows up in the dance classroom when students or their parents expect teachers to entertain and please their children instead of preparing them to be the best dancers they can be.

We need to adapt our teaching to an extent. But we do not need to, nor should we, give in to every transformation that has taken place outside the ballet classroom. We must pursue the goal of leading students to take ownership of their dancing, where they can understand and continue this beautiful tradition we call ballet, and where they choose to study it because they respect and love it on their own terms. As teachers, we must start early in giving students a sense of the history and culture of ballet so they know they're carrying on an exceptional, centuries-old tradition. We must communicate with students and their parents about the norms, etiquette, and requirements of training—what it takes to be a successful ballet student and professional performer. Ballet is a unique, regal, beautiful, and meaningful performing art. We must set this tone and design the ballet classroom as a sacred space where students can enter and leave the details of their daily lives outside.

Our role as teachers is bursting with purpose. We have a job to do, and it's a big one! Children, teens, and young adults rely on us to lead them in the right direction. Many of their future careers depend on it. First and foremost, we must be their teacher, not their friend.

Kindness and inspiration are wonderful. Do you love ballet? Let them know! Do you have giant, amazing dreams for them? Let them know they can reach those dreams and that you believe in them. Yet remember that chumminess with students is unimportant at best and can be detrimental to their learning at worst. We must strike a balance between setting clear standards and maintaining them, while also being an ally to our students. No, we oughtn't walk around with a cane and smack students on their misbehaving body parts. But we can still design a disciplined and ambition-driven training environment. The following concepts and methods will help you create a productive, energetic, and focused classroom.

Classroom Tone and Management

The classroom is where we shepherd talent and ambition, where students train, and where the very origins of performing are learned. So, the atmosphere of every classroom and the structure of each ballet class is essential.

From the beginning—when students are seven or eight years old—we should help them appreciate that they are practicing an art form created hundreds of years ago by royalty in a faraway land. The youngest students may not be old enough to understand or memorize the details of the history of ballet. Still, they can certainly appreciate the regal, proud nature of kings and queens. France and Italy, where ballet originated, are exotic if you are seven and have never been there. Young dancers will instinctively feel important if they know that every time they enter a ballet classroom, they enter a space dedicated to preserving a legendary tradition. As students age, we can fill in the details so these young dancers have a sense of their place in the history of ballet and dance in general. Include studies of historical companies and dancers to inspire them to grand achievements. Encourage these young artists in training to see themselves as part of a whole. This will give them a sense of purpose because they play a role in carrying the art of ballet forward in time.

Also paramount to the ballet classroom is building a sense of decorum, conduct, and professionalism. Part of developing the environment you want is telling your students who *you* are, what you expect of them, and what ballet expects of them. Standards of appearance, conduct, focus, and diligence should be communicated from day one. Whatever your expectations, make sure your students have that information upfront. We all have choices as far as our ground rules are concerned: hair, dress code, noise level, tardiness policy, water break policy, and so forth. If what we expect from our students is made clear to them, they will feel secure in their role.

All teachers must decide for themselves, but here is a list of classroom expectations I set for my students:

Punctuality

1. Arrive on time. Anyone more than fifteen minutes late will be asked to sit and watch class.
2. Late dancers must enter the classroom and stand at the door until invited to join the class.

Attire and Presentation

1. Dancers are expected to dress in uniform: dress code tights and leotard, with hair in a bun for girls/women, and dress code tights and shirt with hair pulled back if needed for boys/men. Ballet or pointe shoes should be worn as required by class.
2. No necklaces, bracelets, or hanging earrings.

Conduct

1. Eyes on the teacher.
2. Silence unless called on.
3. Stand straight without crossing arms or leaning on the barres.
4. Raise a hand for questions.

Attitude

1. Maximum effort is expected with every exercise.
2. Thoughts and energy should be focused on goals for personal improvement and creating beautiful art.
3. Honor the art, the teacher, and other students with diligence, positivity, and perseverance.
4. Know that the dancer you will become is worth the obstacles you face now.
5. Speak only respectful words to the teacher and other students.

The Motivational Classroom

Discipline is essential to ballet training, but it's also crucial to *empower* your students. Give them a sense of influence and providence over their own lives. Discuss with them the power of their brains and bodies. Remind them that not a single professional dancer they idolize or have ever admired was born able to do what they eventually accomplished. Virtuoso dancers were born with talent, but they did not come out of the womb prepared to perform an airborne saut de chat. They chose to set goals and do the work. Professional dancers are not creatures born with magical powers: they are not "other." Professional dancers are humans who, albeit born with some specific physical gifts, pursued their goals from a young age until they got what they wanted. So, tell your students they're never stuck; they always have the power of their mind to make a decision to pursue a greater goal and to do the necessary work.

I use a helpful real-world exercise that I call "Control vs. No Control." Help your students make a list as a class of the things related to ballet over which they have no control, such as the length of their legs or neck, the shape of their hip sockets, and so forth. Next, make a list with them of what they can control: their attitude on any given day, the amount of effort they exert, how much time they put in at home strengthening or stretching. The second list should be longer because, as humans, we have so much control over how we approach any task or goal. Then, create a third list with your students: how they can use the things they can control to improve the things they can't. For example, a dancer with weak feet and ankles can spend ten minutes at home each night doing relevés and working with a Theraband. For another example, students can't control the shape of their hip sockets, which affects turnout, but they can control the amount to which they use their turnout muscles to turn the bones inside their hip sockets and down their legs to maximize their turnout. Ask your students to choose three or four areas they can control and to pursue each as a goal for a semester. By putting in the effort and tracking their progress, they'll learn they each have the ability to change and improve.

Prepare your students to understand that throughout their training, there will be difficult moments. Much of the work will be taxing, challenging, and downright frustrating. Help them know that the difficulty does not mean something has gone wrong or they're doing it wrong. Teach them that when they feel stress and frustration because of the challenge of learning, they can look at that dissatisfaction as a signal that their brain is paying close attention. The irritation and anxiety are akin to bookmarks their minds are setting. Nothing has gone wrong. Everything has gone right because they now know where to focus their efforts. Point out that they are strong enough to persist in that effort: work plus time will yield progress.

You can teach your students that learning something new or correcting something that has been a problem often occurs in three stages. The following is one of the ways I discuss this with my students.

The first stage is the awareness and understanding of what you need to do, fix, or change. It involves listening to descriptions and instructions from a teacher and honest scrutiny of one's own self. We often believe, even feel, we are doing something correctly, when in fact, we are not. For example, I danced with my shoulders up high toward my ears until twelve or thirteen years old. I was often corrected on this problem. I hadn't taken it seriously because I felt I was holding my shoulders in the right place until I did an honest assessment of myself and saw what a mess my shoulders actually looked like. Once I admitted to myself the reality of my technical issue, I was aware of my shoulder alignment problem. Only then was I ready and able to move forward and make the changes that would make me a better dancer.

The second stage is acquiring the knowledge of the correct way to practice a movement and putting into practice this new method every time you do the movement. Again, listening to and following teachers' instructions is the path to learning the correct technique. And practicing it correctly, to the best of your ability every time, is what will train your mental and physical muscles to make this correct approach feel routine to you. It will require much concentration and maybe even some of the struggles discussed above. The truth is that with time and repetition, you will get better at whatever you practice. If you practice executing a ballet step the right way, you will get better at it; then, correctly achieving it will become your permanent custom. However, if you practice your ballet mindlessly and incorrectly, you will get better at carelessness.

The third stage is the actual improvement and eventual mastery. Regular circling back to stages one and two will get you to this mastery of ballet we all desire. It will come in bits and pieces. At the same time, you will improve and master new things! You will have to reassess and focus always on the practicing of your ballet in this meticulous manner.

Help your students to develop these ways of approaching learning, and they will have a strong mentality that will aid them in becoming the best dancers they can be.

Honesty and Tough Love

Looking into the innocent eyes of young students, I can be tempted to praise every movement they attempt. But why would we ever tell even seven-year-olds they're doing something correctly when clearly, they're not? While we're compelled to be kind with these little ones, honest guidance and evaluation are critical to effective learning. Be honest with your students when they're conducting themselves poorly, dancing less than their best, or not living up to the lofty but fair expectations you have set for them. Tell them exactly what they need to change to make a movement correct. They're not stupid and can usually tell when you're lying about their performance. If you're not straight with them, they'll learn from experience not to trust your word. To them, you will have become a lesser educator.

In no way am I saying you should be mentally abusive to your students. The professional dance world is beautiful, but it's also unforgiving; it therefore needs the most effective teachers—and effective teachers are those who combine standards and honesty with the tools for empowerment. Remember that dancers in training also need to hear positive feedback to stay motivated. There is always something to genuinely compliment, whether the effort itself or some other accomplishment in technique or movement.

The best way to strike a balance between tough love and motivation is to know your students well enough to reasonably measure their potential: their short-term potential from day to day, month to month, year to year, and their long-term potential in terms of a career. Communicate the highest possibilities of that potential to them, and make it clear you expect them to meet that standard consistently. If they miss the mark on any given day, tell them how they missed it and what they need to do to hit it. In a related way, tell them when they have done something well. Remind them of their improvements in addition to pointing out their shortcomings. Tell them about the aptitude they have and how their daily work moves them toward their goals.

Class Time Management

I like to begin every year with a review for my students. Take the first two to four weeks of each school year to revisit technical concepts and break down tricky vocabulary. Take class slowly. Although we hope our dancers have danced for most of the summer, they may have had a few weeks off. This review time will remind their muscles what it means to turn out, to plié, etc. After these first few weeks of class, structure class time and precise exercises as you see fit. Would it benefit your students to have five to seven minutes of a particular kind of conditioning at the beginning of each class? How long do you want for barre work? Center? Across the floor? Jumps?

Younger students, seven and eight years old, may begin with classes only one hour in length. They need five minutes of warm-up and conditioning, forty minutes at the barre, and only fifteen minutes in the center. Less-experienced students should spend more time at the barre because they are still learning to dance the basic vocabulary and concepts of ballet. The barre is where students learn the technique of ballet. As students mature and gain experience, classes become longer, and the proportion of barre to center work often shifts because more experienced students require less time learning and repeating new movement at the barre. A ballet class of advanced dancers is typically one and a half to two hours long, with forty-five minutes only of warm-up, conditioning, and barre work. The rest of the class can be dedicated to center and across-the-floor work. The specifics are always at your discretion. Prepare your class and the length of time spent on each portion of class in a manner that reflects what the dancers in front of you need.

Regardless of age and experience, every class should begin with conditioning and a foot warm-up, then move into barre work. Include stretching time for younger and intermediate-level dancers, so they learn how to stretch their bodies properly. Advanced dancers can be given time to stretch on their own. Begin the center with adagio, tendus, and turns before moving into jumps. Always begin the jumps with two-footed jumps to ensure the feet are fully warmed up before executing large jumps on one foot. Include a reverence every single class, even if it's simply a curtsy and thank you, to underscore the tradition, graciousness, and grandeur of ballet.

Thematic Goals and Expectations

Know what you want to work on with each group of students for the week, the month, the year. For example, you may want to use the first month or two to focus on turnout, arabesques, and using the feet in jumps. Develop your classes with those targets in mind. Create a grand allegro and other class combinations that incorporate the month's specific goals. Work backward from there to create barre and center exercises that build toward the grand allegro movements and address the technique and musicality behind these objectives.

Our students must be pushed to execute every classroom combination and movement correctly in myriad measures: classical sense of presence, classical lines, technical strength and precision, knowledge of history and vocabulary, flexibility, musicality, and artistry. A successful class encompasses all these elements during every school year and most of these elements during every class. Today's world of quickly measured success and competition makes it tempting and easy for ballet teachers to give in to the demand to teach advanced vocabulary and choreography to young dancers and skim over many of the details of the crucial elements mentioned here. This is a bad idea that will lead to poor classical performance of the vocabulary at best and injuries due to weakness and bad habits at worst. Especially in their early years of study, dancers must be given the time and space to grasp and eventually master classical ballet's vocabulary, technique, and artistry. Ballet is a scrumptious meal cooked slowly in a crockpot, not a quick, frozen dinner heated in the microwave.

Technique and Consistency

Emphasize that proper technique is a requisite element of being a ballet dancer or any other kind of concert dance performer. Only through attaining correct, clean technique can a dancer create the beautiful lines of classical ballet.

Multiple ballet techniques and styles are taught around the world and within the United States: Cecchetti, Vaganova, Royal Academy of Dance (RAD), Balanchine, Cuban—I could go on. There's even an "American" technique, which, at its best, incorporates thoughtful choices, pulling the most effective components from other techniques into one solid technical structure. Techniques and methods come in and out of fashion. Each has value and strength in what it emphasizes.

A plié is a plié, across the board. The basic vocabulary remains the same across techniques, even though there are different details regarding how the foot works in tendu, how the arms are held, or even few vocabulary differences. What's important is the teacher's knowledge, ability, and understanding of how to apply *consistent* technique within a school to create a coherent foundation.

Conscientiously choose the details of which technique you are using and teaching your students. The same technique and style should be trained on the whole at your school through at least an intermediate level. If you elect to blend elements from more than one official ballet technique in order to create your own, be consistent with your choices. This congruity helps create strong dancers who know who they are. It allows students to build upon what they've learned from day to day. As they gain experience and mature, this consistency will help them develop a solid foundation they can take anywhere in the world—summer intensives, professional companies, professional training schools—and adapt.

Rigorous effort and insistence on meticulous technique are crucial for all dancers. But teaching American bodies in American schools is sometimes different from teaching in other countries. Some countries have state-sponsored schools where dancers are not only auditioned, but also measured, X-rayed, and seen by doctors before being invited to study dance. We don't have that in the United States or many other western countries, and we wouldn't want that anyway. But this does mean we're often teaching bodies that probably don't have naturally ideal turnout, flexibility, or shape. Our job is to teach the bodies in front of us. In other words, we must teach our students the anatomy and logistics behind ballet movement so they can knowledgeably create classical lines with the awareness that comes with understanding the "how."

An ancillary note here: Yes, maintaining one technique of daily training for your dancers is essential for developing accomplished and confident classical dancers. Nonetheless, exposing them to other techniques on occasion will ensure your dancers do not become rigid, losing the ability to adapt to alternative approaches. These two goals may seem at odds; they are not. Educate your students that there are valid ballet techniques and styles beyond what they practice in their school, and that they will be expected to adapt throughout their career as a dancer. You can accomplish this in various ways.

First, discuss the issue with them even when they are young and still practicing only one unvarying technique in daily classes. For example, tell them, "We do frappé from a flexed foot and brush the floor; however, in the Vaganova technique, there is no brush on the floor. You may be asked to do that someday." You can even spend an occasional day having them try the different methods. Later, when the dancers reach an intermediate-advanced level, incorporate weekly classwork that offers them varied methods, techniques, and styles.

Another vital part of this adaptability and ability to move in various ways is having your dancers take dance classes other than ballet classes. Today's professional ballet training should include jazz, modern, and contemporary movement—not daily like ballet, but at least once per week. Today, all professional ballet companies perform a repertoire that crosses the boundaries to include dancing outside the classical realm. Ensure that your dancers are accustomed to a wide variety of movement styles in addition to their ballet training. It may help them get a job one day.

The Relationship Between the Barre Work and the Center Work

Barre work creates center work. Ballet students learn the technique of their dancing at the barre. Include exercises at the barre that teach your students how to execute the specifics of the ballet vocabulary. Communicate to your students the relationship between particular barre exercises and their center work counterparts. For example, learning the control of a controlled fondu from a relevé teaches a dancer how to control the landing from jumps. Another example is battement en clôche (often referred to as balancoire). The brushing from the back, through first, to the front teaches dancers the beginning of many ballet steps: brisé, grand jeté, and grand fouetté sauté, etc. Consider your barre as the development stage of what our students will do in class each day. It serves not only as a warmup but also as instruction for center work.

Communicating to Instruct

Too many teachers command without offering detailed guidance. They tell students to "pull up," "point your feet," or "turn out," without explaining to their dancers which muscles to use and how to make those movements happen. But we can't expect students to intuitively know how dance elements work correctly in the body. So, when it comes to technical instruction, it's crucial to teach your students the logistics and how-to of alignment/center/core, pulling up, turning out, knee placement, arm placement, upper-body alignment, flexibility and extension, and pointing and otherwise using the feet. *(See Chapter 2 for a closer examination of these elements.)*

Remember that we're teaching human beings, and not all humans learn the same way. Nor will they all progress at the same speed. So why should we have only one way of teaching or describing? A great teacher once told me that as a teacher, I should be able to explain every dance step or concept in at least three different ways because people absorb information differently. Some learn through observing a demonstration. Some learn through a verbal, logistical explanation of the step-by-step movement. Others learn by hearing a description and then experiencing how something should feel. And some need another person to physically place their arm or foot where it needs to be. The best ballet teachers provide all of these options.

We teachers must offer explanations that engage the minds and bodies of our students. Some teachers demonstrate every movement and rely on the students' abilities to imitate what they see. My experience has taught me that demonstrating can be a helpful tool, especially with beginner students, but it is not a sufficient mechanism to train dancers. Problems arise when students don't understand what they're watching because they don't know *how* the demonstrator is making something happen—like extending the leg high. Inexperienced dancers will often feel as if they're physically executing what they saw someone else do, even when they're not coming close to it because they don't yet have the necessary body awareness or technical strength and understanding. For instance, they will lift from the quads and pull the hip up to get a high extension rather than holding the body in alignment, rotating the hips and leg muscles, and lifting from underneath.

Another means of teaching is to break down steps and technical concepts verbally. Many teachers explain out loud to their dancers exactly what goes where and how it should feel. These teachers discuss anatomy, physics, and physical mechanics. And they often use visual metaphors. Here's a list of some I've found to be especially effective, from tips for the youngest students up through more advanced levels:

- Your belly button is friends with your nose and wants to go visit your nose for a chat. (This helps young dancers lift their abs before they understand musculature.)

- Imagine that your hips and pelvis are a bowl of cereal sitting atop your legs. Don't tilt your cereal bowl forward or backward, lest you spill Fruit Loops all over the floor.

- To point your feet and maintain energy through your feet and toes, imagine that your legs and feet are magic wands that can shoot magical sparks out of your toes.

- When your arms are in first or second position, visualize a cloud under your elbow and don't allow your elbows to sink into the cloud.

- Your arms should move through your positions as though your bones were hollow.

- Knit your abs closer to your lowest rib. At the same time, allow your ribs to rest in place.

- To combat the habit of sinking back into the ribs, imagine your back as rib, space, rib, space, rib, space.

- Imagine your legs are two barbershop poles: the red and white type that rotate. To help turnout, visualize the poles turning away from each other from within your hip sockets all the way down to the floor.

- When standing flat, try to feel as if you're about to relevé, to keep the weight off your heels.

- When you tendu or dégagé back, the little toe should be the part of your body farthest behind you.

- In retiré (passé), lift the heel to the belly button, as opposed to trying to lift the thigh.

- For greater ease with extension in grand battement, push down through the floor as you begin the battement, then release the working leg on the way up; the momentum will help you.

- For a more solid supporting leg, visualize the balls of your feet reaching through the floor when on relevé. Do the same on pointe by imaging that your big toe reaches into the earth.

- A pirouette is nothing more than a relevé holding still, which you do all the time—as a balance. If you have the basics of balancing well, you can turn well.

- To improve all turns, rotate with the second side of your back, being aware of its moving in space. If you are turning to the right, think about the left side of your back turning toward the right.

- To improve your grand jetés (leaps), move in the following order. Start first with a fast grand battement or développé front that you hold out in front of you, and then push off your back leg. Do not start both the front and back leg movements at the same time.

As necessary as verbal cues are, students' cognitive understanding of a piece of classical vocabulary doesn't necessarily translate to kinesthetic understanding. They need to be physically aware of what their bodies should *feel* like upon executing specific movements. So, it's important to connect verbal instruction with exercises emphasizing correct muscle usage—exercises that build the physical habits and muscle memory needed to achieve the classical lexicon, aesthetic, and technique.

Bottom line: the most efficacious way to educate your students is to draw on all the above methods collectively, in balance with one another.

Beyond Technique

Address artistry and musicality in the classroom. Start with young dancers by giving them opportunities to "free dance." Play music with multiple tempos, dynamics, and styles. Allow them to dance around the classroom, asking them to show how the music makes them feel and what kind of adjectives are in the music: smooth, sharp, slow, quick. As dancers advance in years and technical experience, they use a diverse range of tempos and dynamics in class combinations. Musicality, artistry, and technique go hand in hand. Dancers must have clean lines to communicate their intention clearly. They must also have a sense of presence and the ability to share emotions with the audience. Teach your dancers to keep in mind a story. That story can be a complex story of love or redemption. Or it can be simple, as in the beauty of curved lines. Work with them on the "why" of their dancing as much as on the "what and how." Develop their artistry along with their technique, not as an afterthought.

Advocate for your students to watch performances of ballet and all types of dance often. Part of developing artists is encouraging them to see as much live performance as possible. Performances kindle discovery in dancers of all ages and levels, and your students will bring those stimulating ideas back into the classroom. They'll observe how professional dancers use music, spacing, the energy of other dancers, and emotions as part of their performances. Encourage your students to try out some of the musical and artistic choices they enjoyed. Allow them to be inspired, and then adapt their own sense of artistic choice.

Readiness for Pointe Work

Getting it right—knowing when a dancer is ready for pointe is crucial for numerous reasons. First and foremost, dancing on pointe before a student is physically and mentally equipped is unsafe. Injuries of all types abound under these circumstances: broken bones from falling, tendonitis, and sprained ankles, to name a few. Adjacent to the safety issue is the fact that, even at its best, dancing on pointe too early can create bad habits that hinder a dancer's progression. The truth is that waiting until a student has developed sufficient technique, physical strength, and mental focus to work correctly on pointe may require an extra year or two of training before undertaking pointe work. Nonetheless, the dancer who waits will ultimately advance faster and reach a more skillful level of dancing.

How do we know, then, when a student is ready for pointe work? There are criteria that we can use to evaluate a student to determine preparedness for pointe work. These include:

- Previous experience—at least three years of training two to three days per week.

- Time and commitment, history of willingness to commit enough hours per week to study.

- Maturity and focus.

- Basic mastery of fundamental technique.

- Core alignment.

- Foot and ankle strength.

- Knee and foot alignment when turning out.

Setting an Example

We need to be admirable examples of the presence and effort we demand from our students. Each day, consider how you behave and how you present yourself in the classroom. There are times when everything in my day has gone wrong, and I may be near tears ten minutes before I walk into the studio. What do I have to do there and then? Put it away. All the while I'm in front of my students, I must leave other distractions behind and focus on the task at hand. We set high expectations for decorum and urge our students to leave the outside world behind once they walk into the classroom. We, therefore, owe them the same.

Parent Education

Include parents and family in the education and training of dancers. Without the support of family, becoming a professional dancer is impossible. We don't need to teach our students' parents classical technique, but we do need to teach them all that is involved in becoming a ballet dancer. Communicate routinely and with a consistent message. Explain ballet etiquette to everyone who registers at your school. Emphasize the formality of ballet and the importance of pulling back hair and following the dress code to help maintain focus in the classroom and allow the teacher to observe the musculature of dancers. Advise parents that there is no benefit to beginning pointe work too early. And set clear expectations about the hours required to study ballet, pointe, and other forms of dance, as well as the hours necessary for rehearsals and student performances, which are fundamental to becoming a professional dancer.

Make a determined effort to bring the parents along for this journey to help advance their children's talent and efforts effectively. Hold meetings, send emails, and organize group outings to professional performances and workshops. Invite families to research the training schedules at preeminent classical ballet schools around the world for comparison. Bring professional dancers to speak at your school to share their training experiences. Parental understanding fosters support, which will help build a professional, growth-oriented atmosphere throughout your school.

Diversifying the Classroom

How do we make the classroom more inclusive? Many teachers, myself included, are grappling with this issue. The ballet world at large is only beginning to address its insufficiencies honestly in this area. Ballet has often failed to embrace humanity's beautiful variety: differences in skin color, ethnicity, body type, and experience. We can retain the valued foundations of this art form— the technique, the storytelling, the music—while also acknowledging that our world is overdue for renovation. For ballet to remain relevant, we must encourage a more expansive vision of who can be a dancer, and make the classroom and the stage an inviting place for all: allowing for different body types, promoting attire (costumes, tights, shoes) that reflects non-white dancers' skin tones, and casting dancers of color in leading roles.

We must also promote non-white artists and administrators into executive leadership within ballet schools, companies, and other arts organizations so that impactful decisions in the art world stem from a comprehensive scope of humans. This change will also give young children a diverse group of leaders and role models to observe.

We must also confront the intertwining of economics and inequality. Rigorous ballet study and performances are expensive. That truth alone makes it impossible for every person who would like to participate in the art form to engage in it. Minority populations are affected by this reality more than others. Scholarships, mentorship, and free performances would improve this obstacle.

Only when you have diversity from the inside will a broader, more diverse audience be drawn to ballet.

The Recreational Dancer

Recreational dancers are those who attend class only once or twice per week for different reasons. They may simply love their time in class, or they may appreciate the physical fitness ballet brings. Treat these dancers with as much respect as you do your students in rigorous, daily training. Set high expectations for them regarding diligence, technique, and musicality. Too often I see teachers lower their quality of instruction when working with hobbyist ballet students. That's ridiculous. Ballet is still ballet and deserves to be taught properly. And these students are still fully capable of hard work and learning. You'll have different long-term expectations for what their bodies will be able to master and what their careers might be, but they deserve your best as a teacher, regardless of their goals.

School Directorship

If you own or direct a ballet training school, run your school well. Be organized about communication, scheduling, finances, and marketing. Besides the obvious benefits of maintaining a successful business, keeping your clients' confidence is also important. If they witness frequent mistakes in running your business, they'll have reason to doubt you and become frustrated. Any negative associations with the school as a whole can bleed into parents' thoughts and trust in your ability to train their children.

Select the teachers who educate in your school carefully. They represent you. Choose teachers whose education, experience, and teaching philosophies align with or complement yours, and who bring to the school quality knowledge. I have found that discussing with them my expectations as far as supporting the school's teaching technique, style, and classroom decorum *before* they begin teaching for the school to be helpful. Don't stop there. Communicate clearly and thoroughly with your teaching staff: keep them updated on every plan and decision that affects them. Failing to do this creates confusion in the teachers that will bleed into a lack of confidence in your establishment.

Ballet Competitions

Ballet competitions of all levels of prestige and seriousness have become super popular in the past decade. In many ways, these competitions can be tremendously valuable to the dancer participating. But I'm of two minds about these.

The case in favor: Having a goal like a prestigious competition can generate drive and ambition in some dancers. I've had students push themselves because they were motivated to place in a ballet competition, who then maintained that work ethic beyond the competition, as they saw how successful the hard work made them. The time spent in private coaching developing precision and artistry will help most dancers grow. Any time on stage is added performance experience, which makes for a better performer. Nerves run spectacularly high in competitions, and learning to conquer those nerves carries over into all performances. And all the extra time and effort spent toiling to perfect the craft and art of ballet outside of class is a great tool in the life of a dancer.

The time spent at these competitions can be beneficial as well, particularly for dancers from small schools. Students who aspire to professional careers will profit from observing what else is out there, as far as what a pre-professional ballet dancer is expected to be capable of. It can be an eye-opening experience. Young dancers have the opportunity to meet new dance peers and to develop connections. Participants at major ballet competitions are often seen by teachers and directors of large professional training schools. They can be offered scholarships even when they don't win anything directly in the competition. Last, students can actually learn from their failures. If they're willing to accept a poor performance and then use any negative feelings as a catalyst to push themselves to do better next time, they'll work even more diligently in the future. At that point, it's our job as teachers and coaches, to be honest about their underperformance, remind them they can use it as a tool to change their habits, and teach them what they need to focus on next. I have watched this happen to my students numerous times. Resilience is a powerful tool.

Then there's the case against: For the dance student, massive success at a ballet competition can lead to a "star mentality." These students may come to believe they're more important than their peers and therefore cease to work well with others. They can also begin to slack off in their classwork and rehearsals if winning has caused them to believe they've already accomplished their mission. It's our job as teachers to combat this. Nobody is more important than anyone else in the ballet class today, no matter what happened yesterday.

Another negative of ballet competitions is the added expense of coaching time, costumes, travel, and entry fees. Not every family can afford this considerable expense. Teachers must educate their students that many professional dancers who never competed in a ballet competition still make a living today. Such competition does not promise a ballet career; nor does the lack of it exclude a ballet career.

Finally, does competition turn ballet into a sport when it should remain an art form? It certainly can. If you teach your students and their families that the only successful outcome is winning, then competition indeed reduces ballet to a sport. Why not teach them, instead, that these competitions are experiences and tools valuable to the development of a dancer? Base success on technical, artistic, and personal growth—not tricks and medals.

Chapter 2

Proper Technique as a Foundation

Technique is one of the foundations of classical ballet and most other dance forms. Entire books have been written on classical technique alone. In this chapter, I address technical and further concepts I've found to be fundamental in the life of a dancer, and which should be covered in the ballet classroom. I define and describe center alignment, weight distribution upon the feet on and off pointe, supporting-side control, turnout, use of the knees and lower legs, pointing of the feet, how to use the feet from the floor, extensions, flexibility, coordination, and musicality and artistry. *(Later chapters, such as the chapter on conditioning, include more detailed methods of working with students on these concepts.)*

A helpful way to discuss the technical elements described in this chapter is to ask your students to think of their body as a puzzle, in which parts are placed into the correct position but do not need to be squeezed. They can arrange their muscles, tendons, and body parts; they do not need to tighten to the point of constraining their mobility. This metaphor offers dancers a visual aid that can reduce tension and increase ease of movement.

Alignment

First things first! Dancers must learn proper alignment of their center, core, torso, and hips. Start by talking to them about what's important to focus on. Some teachers teach to squeeze or tuck the bottom. I disagree. Squeezing the bottom leads to tightness and lack of mobility. Tucking the tailbone creates a weak center. Instead, teach your dancers to align the front of their body: top of the thighs, hip flexors, front of the hip bone, and abs, all stacked on top of one another. The abdominal muscles do this work. Dancers should use their abs to pull their hip flexors up and long in order to create a straight line in the front. If dancers engage their abdominal muscles to lift their belly buttons up closer to their lowest rib and align the front of their hips directly underneath the front of their ribs, they will not arch their backs. With the front of their hip bones lifted up and forward, their pelvises will be in neutral alignment. No need to try to tuck the bottom under—it can simply work to lengthen down.

Look out for dancers who make the mistake of pulling their ribs up and out in this effort. They need to learn to tighten and lift abs while keeping their ribs in place. I have found an image that helps many of my students: a sunflower! Tell them, "Press the balls of your feet into and through the floor like the roots reaching down into the earth. Pull your knees and abs up tall like the strong, upright stem of a sunflower. Then allow your chest, collarbone, shoulders, and face to be the beautiful blossom of the sunflower, *resting* open in the sun." Leaving out technical instructions, this visual allows students to ground themselves and lift their centers without pulling up their chest and shoulders.

Weight Distribution

Dancers carry their weight lifted and forward on their feet. The details of weight distribution vary depending on how they're standing. While they're standing flat, have your students press their metatarsals into the floor as their heels rest on the floor. Their little toes must reach to the floor while standing flat, without carrying any weight. On relevé, the little toes will not touch the floor; teach your students to place all of their weight into a triangle on the bottom of the foot: the big toe, the metatarsal of the big toe, and the metatarsal of the middle toe. Last, there is the distribution of weight while standing on pointe. Teach your dancers to carry all of their weight on pointe on their first three toes, with most of it on the big toes.

Supporting-Side Control

"Your supporting side should be more tired than your working leg!" My students hear this refrain all the time. An integral part of center alignment is holding the supporting side: a dancer's supporting side (standing leg side) is their base. Teach your students to transfer their weight forward over the ball of the foot of their supporting side before any movement of the working leg is initiated. Instill in them that they must maintain the alignment of their standing side as a priority. They should feel able to throw their working leg around and sustain a solid balance on their supporting (standing) side.

Turnout and Rotation

Turnout is another foundational element of a ballet dancer's technique. Again, your words matter here. First and foremost, teach your students that "turn out" is a verb, not a noun. Turning out is an action, something we do. Some people are born with more natural turnout. But naturally endowed or not, every student can learn to use the appropriate muscles in the torso, hips, backs, and insides of the thighs to turn out. Everyone can grow their turnout by using the correct muscles and tendons and by stretching the correct areas.

Once more, offer visuals. Two old-time barbershop poles, the ones with the red and white stripes, both rotating away from each other. A set of gears with intersecting teeth, turning in opposite directions. The internal anatomy of muscles wrapping outward around the bone and working to move the bones. Any of these examples can help the concept of turning out click for a student. *(In Chapter 4, I describe several exercises for improving turnout using the correct muscles.)*

Look out for the dancer who wants to turn out too much—a habit known as forcing turnout. Teach students to use the correct muscles to their maximum ability while maintaining proper alignment. The position they reach is their current turnout. Many students want to force their feet out past what they can hold correctly. It's imperative to be vigilant about correcting this. When students force their turnout, they often roll in on their arches and can't keep their hips and pelvis properly aligned. At best, this creates a weak line. At worst, it can cause significant injury.

Knees and Feet

Knees and feet are crucial to the ballet dancer's line. Teach your students what a straight knee is and how to develop and attentively use strong, well-arched feet.

Knees can be tricky. A dancer must have enough strength in the quads and flexibility in the hamstrings to properly straighten the knee. The goal is to pull the kneecaps up without locking the backs of the knees. In Chapter 4, I describe specific conditioning exercises for this kind of strength and flexibility. I also detail an exercise to help students with hyperextended knees find what a straight knee should feel like when it is the supporting leg. What you don't want is to have the hyperextended knee locked back in a fashion that curves the leg past a straight line, shifts the body weight back, and creates instability. You want to have both the kneecap and the lower quads pulled up to create a straight line along the leg and keep the weight forward. It's vital to address hyperextended knees to minimize the chance of injury to lower legs, feet, and ankles.

Be sure that every class also includes a few exercises for strengthening articulation of the feet. You can do this as part of conditioning and also include plenty of exercises to develop the feet at the barre, such as tendus and relevés.

Using the Feet to Initiate Movement

"Dance from your feet!" Another refrain my students hear daily. In addition to completing a beautiful line with strong and well-arched feet, dancers need to learn to travel through space from their feet. Teach your students to use the floor to push through, push off, roll off, roll onto, etc. One important example of this concept is jumping. Dance students have a tendency to use their upper bodies and try to lift themselves into the air when they are learning to jump, when they should be pushing from underneath and initiating the movement from their feet. Using the foot movement of temps lié, ask your students to pay attention to how they use their feet and toes to push their weight from one foot to the other. They can use that same movement—pushing from their feet to initiate jumps and then continue through the legs as they push up. In the end, every movement begins with the foot shaping, pushing, or brushing through the floor. Give them an abundance of foot warm-ups, tendus, dégagés, and relevés. Include the feet conditioning exercises I outline in Chapter 4.

Flexibility and Extension

Flexibility is a hot topic in today's dance world. How much is too much? All teachers must make their own decisions about how best to draw this line. I teach first and foremost that dancers must be flexible because it makes creating classical lines easier. Stretching feet, legs, hips, backs, shoulders—it's all important. But overstretching to an extreme is dangerous. Ballet dancers needn't be contortionists. For example, there is no need to practice extreme over-splits. If someone is in a split without any strain to the muscles, it's acceptable to put one or both feet on a small foam block only three to four inches high, but that is the most necessary. I stress that it should only occur when a student is already easily in a split without feeling any pain. Anything more extreme is dangerous; it could cause injury by ripping a muscle or a tendon. Even when not causing immediate damage, continued overstretching to the point of pain can make tendons loose, weak, and unsupported.

Extension itself stems only partially from flexibility: both strength and mechanics of the movement pattern are equally important. Give your students barre and conditioning exercises that build strength in the muscles needed to hold the legs properly. And teach your dancers the movement pattern of the leg through a développé, grand battement, or battement lent. The goal is to develop the leg through specific points and benchmarks along the way, not simply to throw it up high. *(I detail the correct pattern for développé later, in Chapter 3.)*

Coordination

Coordination serves to bring connectedness and smoothness to a dancer's movement. Some people are born with immense coordination. We can help others to develop theirs. Work with dancers on which body parts initiate movement. Remind them to dance from their feet, and teach them which other body parts set us in motion. For example, dancers often forget to turn with their backs during pirouettes and other turning movements. In this case, have them consciously move their backs through space as they turn. Remind them to take the working side of their backs with them.

Coordination can be improved further by teaching about the distribution of one's weight throughout movement. As dancers are given more complex combinations in class, be explicit about where the weight of their bodies should be to proceed smoothly to the next movement. And provide them with something that travels throughout the space in each class—at least one "dancey" combination, even during slow, technical classes. The repeated practice of just doing it helps build coordination as well.

Musicality and Artistry

Musicality and artistry are not categorical elements of technique. But they must be taught in the classroom alongside technique, not left only to time on stage. Engage your students in the joy, work, and practice of musicality and artistry in the classroom from the beginning. Classical ballet is a performance art. We should be practicing the performance part of it at all times. Work with your students on developing a sense of presence that sends energy all the way to the back row of a theater. Teach them that their sense of presence comes through their eyes and collarbone. They should be aware of sending out energy from these points. Encourage your students to think in terms of storytelling. This can mean many things: a complex tale of love betrayed, a physical illustration of the music, the story of a particular feeling or shape. Whatever the case, teach your students to have something they're dancing *about*—even in the classroom. Then give your students as many performance opportunities as possible. Time on stage is essential to cultivating artistry.

Chapter 3

Let's Talk About Fifth

Plenty of classical steps are misunderstood or taught too quickly and, therefore, are performed incorrectly or poorly. Teaching these steps with precision and care is crucial, in the interest of injury prevention and correct accomplishment of each movement. In this chapter, you'll find a list of the movements I've seen are most frequently executed poorly: fifth position, demi-plié, tendu, closing into fifth position from second, retiré, développé, assemblé, jeté, arabesque, piqué, grand jeté développé (saut de chat), pas de chat, and arms à la seconde (plus other positions involving support of the elbows). I also discuss the correct placement of the feet and pointe shoes while standing on pointe. Photos illustrate each step and indicate the correct and incorrect version. My goals are to address key points I often observe being implemented improperly and to describe and demonstrate (in the photos) the correct mechanical and technical methods of performing each step.

Fifth Position

"There is ONLY ONE correct fifth position." This refrain probably haunts my students' dreams. To be clear: a precise fifth position will not be strictly the same on every body, but there is only one correct version for each dancer. Every time a dancer closes into fifth position, they must go all the way to the best fifth their body can form without compromising core alignment or technique. This means starting with proper alignment of the hips, abs, ribs, back, and chest as the foundation, and then maximizing turnout using the correct muscles. Kneecaps are also pulled up, and weight is off the heels. Legs are crossed enough so the feet are crossed in front of each other, front heel in front of back toes, and front toes in front of back heel. Center and core alignment and the distribution of weight on the feet are priorities; everything else is executed to the best of the dancer's ability while maintaining the correct placement. Nothing less than this—for example, crossing or turning out the legs less than a dancer's capacity while in proper alignment, or forcing the feet to cross and turn out while allowing the pelvis to tilt and the ankles to roll in—should ever be considered fifth position. *See Figure 1, Figure 2, Figure 3, Figure 4*

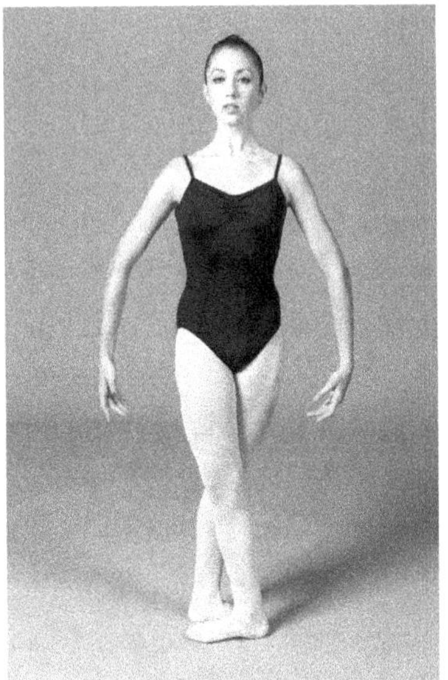

Figure 1. Correct fifth position. Legs and feet are crossed.

Figure 2. Correct fifth position. Legs and feet are crossed.

Figure 3. Correct hip alignment in fifth position.

Figure 4. Incorrect hip alignment in fifth position.
Note the tilted pelvis and hips.

Demi-Plié

If a dancer cannot demi-plié correctly, they cannot dance well. End of story. Most of the classical ballet vocabulary begins with a demi-plié. (The rest initiates with a tendu, discussed next in this chapter.)

Demi-plié, literally translated, means half-bent or half-folded; it does not mean to go down. The tendency to interpret simply a down and up motion is wrong.

Figure 5. Correct demi-plié.

Figure 6. Incorrect demi-plié. Note the knees and ankles rolling forward.

Demi-plié is about rotating the legs, opening the hips, and bending the knees. The fact that your body happens to get closer to the floor is a *result* of the motion, not the goal.

A dancer needs to begin a first-position demi-plié with the body in correct alignment. Ensure that the weight is off the heels even though the heels are touching the floor and will remain on the floor throughout the entire demi-plié. Begin by rotating the legs within the hip sockets, all the way down through the backs of the thighs, then allow that motion to bend your knees.

First, imagine your body as a pulley, with your back being pulled down as your front is pulled up through the kneecaps and abdominal muscles. As you lower due to your knees bending, applying an opposite motion also pulls your belly button up. Continue to bend your knees until you feel as though your heels may come off the floor; they should feel as if they're almost hanging atop the ground. Open your hips and your knees as wide as you can without turning out your feet any further.

Figure 7: Incorrect demi-plié. Note the tilted pelvis and hips.

For a useful visual, think of a book: it's helpful to imagine your knees and the front of your hips as pages being pulled and opened in opposite directions, and the middle of your body as the book's spine. Another visual is to imagine you're in a pool of water. Keep your upper body lifted as though you're floating in the water, trying to stay afloat while holding a beachball under the water with your legs. On the way up, keep your knees and hips even more open and wide than they were on the way down, and keep the balls of the feet pressed through the floor and the heels lightly on the floor. *See Figure 5, Figure 6, Figure 7*

Tendu

The first motion of a tendu is to transfer one's weight onto the supporting leg—specifically, over and forward, onto the ball of the big toe and the next two toes of the supporting leg. For tendu in all directions, the inside of the working thigh initiates the motion by rotating from underneath the leg. Next, lead the tendu with the correct part of the working foot and leg. In tendu devant, the inside of the ankle bone and inner thigh both reach forward. In tendu à la seconde, the first three toes and the rotation of the inner thigh begin the brush. In tendu derrière, the working leg's little toe reaches back as the metatarsals of the first three toes start to push down and back.

The supporting side should do at least as much work as the working leg. It's tempting to allow the supporting side to twist, rock, or lean as one performs a tendu. Working the entire supporting side to hold it in place is more important the any-thing one can do with the working leg. Alignment, turnout, and weight distribution must be worked and reworked on the standing leg while executing any step in the ballet vocabulary. This concept of rotation from underneath the working leg while maintaining the correct standing position in the supporting leg—by committing to supporting-side engagement—becomes even more critical in movement where the working leg lifts off the floor. It's imperative to gain this strength and skill in tendu in order to use it in more complex movement.

Now, the foot. When moving the working leg in tendu, it's important to articulate and roll the foot on the way out and back in: heel toe, toe heel. Always. This motion develops strength and coordination of the feet. As a dancer works through the ball of their foot in tendu, they should push the ball down through the floor without transferring any weight onto the foot. Once in full tendu, in à la quatrième devant, and à la seconde, the tip of the big toe is ideally all that touches the floor. In tendu à la quatrième derrière, in arabesque, the inside tip of the big toe is ideally all that touches the floor. Upon the working leg's closing, the weight should most often go back to being equally distributed between the metatarsals of both feet; however, when executing multiple fast tendus, it's better to keep the weight on the supporting leg even upon closing. *See Figure 8, Figure, 9, Figure 10, Figure 11, Figure 12, Figure 13*

Tendu Devant

Figure 8. Correct tendu to fourth devant rolling through the foot along the way.

Figure 9. Correct lengthened tendu to fourth devant.

Tendu à la Seconde

Figure 10. Correct tendu à la seconde rolling through the foot along the way.

Figure 11. Correct lengthened tendu à la seconde.

Tendu to Fourth Derrière

Figure 12. Correct tendu derrière rolling through the foot along the way.

Figure 13. Correct lengthened tendu to fourth derrière.

Closing Into Fifth From Second

When a dancer executes a tendu à la seconde from fifth position or closes the leg into fifth from second, they must pass through first position—regardless of whether they are closing fifth front or back. Otherwise, they are doing a rond de jambe. *See Figure 14, Figure 15, Figure 16*

Figure 14. Begin in tendu à la seconde.

Figure 15. Note the correct passage through first position before legs and feet close into fifth position.

Figure 16. End by sliding to fifth position after passing through first position.

Retiré (Passé)

I frequently observe dancers pulling their knee or thigh as high as possible while executing a retiré, resulting in a compromise of the supporting side with tilted or rocked hips. Actively lifting your heel high instead of your thigh will result in a better-aligned position while maintaining the height of the leg. Retiré begins with the transfer of weight from the ball of both feet forward over the ball of just the supporting leg's big toe. The working leg then rotates open as the foot peels off the floor into a coupé position, wrapped or unwrapped. It's important to feel the working heel moving under and up toward the belly button. From here, feel the heel being driven into the belly button while the outside of the little toe remains attached to the front of the leg. The supporting side must persist in lifted alignment the entire time. Take note that it's the working-leg heel that lifts high, not the thigh or the knee, and this helps to create a position with square hips. The effort in the working thigh is to rotate and keep the knee open, not to lift. *See Figure 17, Figure 18, Figure 19*

Figure 17. Correct position from the front.　　Figure 18. Correct position from the side.　Figure 19. Incorrect position. Note the lifted working hip.

Développé

Dancers periodically bend their leg and hoist it up without knowledgeably proceeding through the correct path of a développé. Développé means to develop or unfold. When performing a développé, it's necessary to progress through a specific path to accomplish the step properly and create classical lines throughout the movement. It begins with the transfer of weight from the ball of both feet forward over the ball of just the supporting leg. You then follow the steps to create a high retiré position. The working leg remains attached to the supporting leg all the way up to the full retiré before it separates from the supporting leg. The working knee then travels up into a full attitude position before the knee extends straight. In other words, do not separate from the knee before reaching a full retiré, and do not straighten before reaching the full height of attitude. Initiate the movement after your retiré position and into your attitude with the muscles underneath and inside of the working thigh while thinking about keeping the knee open the entire time. Each benchmark along the way must be accomplished before moving on to the next portion of a développé.

See Figure 20, Figure 21, Figure 22, Figure 23, Figure 24, Figure 25, Figure 26, Figure 27, Figure 28, Figure 29, Figure 30, Figure 31

Développé Devant

Figure 20. Correct movement through full retiré.

Figure 21. Correct movement through attitude.

Figure 22. Lengthened développé devant.

Figure 23. Incorrect. Note the separation from the supporting leg before passage through retiré.

Développé à la Seconde

Figure 24. Correct movement through full retiré.

Figure 25. Correct movement through attitude.

Figure 26. Lengthened développé à la seconde.

Figure 27. Incorrect. Note the separation from the supporting leg before passage through retiré.

Développé Derrière (Arabesque)

Figure 28. Correct movement through full retiré.

Figure 29. Correct movement through attitude.

Figure 30. Lengthened développé to arabesque.

Figure 31. Incorrect. Note the separation from the supporting leg before passage through retiré.

Assemblé

The problem I often observe in assemblé is that dancers tend to brush their working leg out as they push off the supporting leg. The working leg is meant to brush out as the supporting leg deepens its demi-plié. Begin each assemblé with both legs going into a demi-plié. As the supporting leg completes the demi-plié, the working leg brushes out to a dégagé position while still in plié. At the same time, you're pushing straight down into the floor with the bottom leg to jump straight up. The working leg closes, or assemblés, into sous-sus at the highest point in the air. Both legs remain in fifth and land together in plié. Assemblé travels directly up and down. There is sideways travel in an assemblé porté. *See Figure 32, Figure 33, Figure 34*

Figure 32. Begin with a brush to second while in plié.

Figure 33. Close to sous-sus with the jump up.

Figure 34. Incorrect. Note the jump while the working leg is still extended in second.

Jeté

As in assemblé, the position of the jeté should be found in the air. One should not wait until landing to coupé the leg. *See Figure 34a*

Figure 34a. Like assemblé, jeté creates the shape in the air.

Arabesque

Because there are multiple varieties of arabesque among the many different techniques, I will not be addressing which is first, second, or third arabesque, etc. I will address the universal aspects of an arabesque needed to do it well.

Arabesque is the position in which the working leg extends behind the shoulder or center of the body. It is a beautiful line when done correctly. To start, the weight moves forward over the ball of the big toe on the supporting leg. During the entirety of the arabesque, the supporting-side hip bone stands lifted and forward, directly above the supporting big-toe metatarsal. In tendu arabesque, both hips should remain square, and the pelvis should not tilt at all. But attempting to keep both hips square once the working leg lifts off the floor above 45 degrees is not helpful. Work instead on maintaining the alignment of the supporting side to include the leg, pelvis, and center. If the supporting side is kept lifted and in alignment, the working side hip cannot move too far. It's attached! Keep the back, ribs, and shoulder of the supporting side aligned as well. They should be opened and connected to the working leg behind them. Another way to think about this is to open the supporting-side shoulder to the working leg. For example, if you are standing on your right leg, the right side of the back, ribs, and shoulders should feel not only lifted tall but also as though they are subtly rotating to the right and reaching for the left heel. The back and ribs on the working-leg side should be elongated, even though it's tempting to pinch them together. Pinching the working side creates an unsightly line, causes pain, and ultimately restricts movement. From this alignment, be sure to keep the working leg straight, knee facing out. *See Figure 35, Figure 36, Figure 37, Figure 38, Figure 39, Figure 40, Figure 41*

Correct Arabesque Alignment

Figure 35. Correct arabesque alignment.

Figure 36. Correct arabesque alignment.

Figure 37. Correct arabesque alignment.

Figure 38. Correct arabesque alignment.

Incorrect Arabesque Alignment

Figure 39. Incorrect. Note the weight back on the heel and the tilted pelvis and back.

Figure 40. Incorrect. Note the weight back on the heel and the tilted pelvis and back.

Figure 41. Incorrect. Note the pinched working side and the crooked shoulders and ribs.

Piqué

The primary problem I witness with piqué is "climbing" onto it. I observe dancers shift their weight as they extend the leg and then reach with the leg, trying to pull themselves up onto pointe. It creates a belabored energy. Piqué needs to happen in one motion altogether—at once. One leg extends while the weight is still fully over the supporting foot in a demi-plié. Then the supporting foot pushes all its weight onto the first leg and cuts directly to whatever position it holds in the piqué. The piqué is landed on, not climbed onto. *See Figure 42, Figure 42a, Figure 43, Figure 44 on the next page.*

Piqué

Figure 42. Extend leg to prepare for piqué.

Figure 42a. Incorrect. Note the weight off the supporting leg and the twisted hips.

Figure 43. Correct piqué alignment.

Figure 44. Incorrect. Note the dancer is not fully over the box and will have to climb up.

Grand Jeté Développé (Saut de Chat)

Grand jeté développé is not just a big jump in which the legs are thrown into a split. Any coordinated, flexible person can do that. In grand jeté développé, the legs follow a specific pattern of developing into the correct movement. It's important to begin with the weight entirely on the pushing leg before taking off. First, a quick développé is executed with the front leg as the back leg begins the push-off. Then, as the first leg is straightening, the second leg pushes hard to jump up into the air and forward while executing a grand battement back. The first leg and foot complete the développé, hold the position, and reach forward before the second leg rises fully behind the dancer. The whole time, the front leg should remain lengthened; the dancer travels not only up but also forward toward the big toe of the extended développé by pushing from the back leg and lifting the pelvis up and forward toward the front leg. Keeping the pelvis up and forward not only propels the dancer high into the air and forward through space, but it also allows the dancer to land on the front foot quietly because their weight is over the front leg. *See Figure 45, Figure 46, Figure 47, Figure 48, Figure 49, Figure 50, Figure 51, Figure 52*

Figure 45. Front leg develops before the back leg pushes off the ground and lifts.

Figure 46. Back leg lifts to complete the saut de chat.

Figure 47. Incorrect. Note the front leg held bent while the back leg extends.

Figure 48. Front leg develops before the back leg pushes off the ground and lifts.

Figure 49. Front leg develops before the back leg pushes off the ground and lifts.

Figure 50. Back leg lifts to complete the saut de chat.

Figure 51. Front leg develops before the back leg pushes off the ground and lifts.

Figure 52. Back leg lifts to complete the saut de chat.

Pas de Chat

Dancers often begin the jump and lift the second leg too late. They execute an incorrect jump in which the first leg is already descending by the time the second leg lifts.

Figure 53. Both legs pull up to retiré at the height of the jump.

There is then no moment when both legs are lifted into a retiré position. It's vital to jump with and lift the second leg as soon as the first leg pulls up, to create a position in the air in which both legs are high in retiré for an instant. Put another way, pas de chat is a movement that should be performed with both legs at once—not one and then the other. The first leg begins scarcely before the second leg, and then they work together in the air and land almost simultaneously. *See Figure 53*

Arms à la Seconde—and Other Positions Involving Support of the Elbows

Maintaining support in the arms is crucial to creating a classical line and to engaging the back. *(In Chapter 4, there's a great exercise that teaches how to feel the proper use of the elbows and arms.)*

The sense of a supported elbow needs to be sustained through all positions of the arms. In second, the arms are held out to the side without allowing the elbows to go behind the ribs. There's a gentle roundness from the shoulders to the tips of the fingers while holding the elbows supported and keeping the same amount of curve through the wrists and fingers. There should not be any extra curving in from the wrist. Nor should there be any drooping of the pinkies. Keep the hand the same height as the wrist. Imagining one long arm from fingertips to fingertips is helpful to engaging the back as well.

Cultivating this support through the elbows and back is important in many classical arm positions. Arms en bas (also bras bas, or preparatory) use the same feeling of support to keep the elbows out and not sinking back. Arms in middle first have the elbows facing out, not down. And arms in fifth use the same feeling of motion through the back and arms to keep the elbows out, not drooping forward. *See Figure 54, Figure 55, Figure 56, Figure 57*

Figure 54. Arms à la seconde.

Figure 55. Incorrect. Note the unsupported, drooping elbows.

Figure 56. Incorrect. Note the drooping little fingers.

Figure 57. Incorrect. Note the lifted fingers.

On Pointe

Dancers on pointe should stand on straight toes within their box, directly on top of the platform. Going too far over the box or standing behind the box is unacceptable.

See Figure 58, Figure 59, Figure 60, Figure 61, Figure 62, Figure 63

Figure 58. On pointe in first position.

Figure 59. Incorrect. Note the dancer is too far over the box and past the platform.

Figure 60. Incorrect. Note the dancer is not on top of the platform and is on the back of the box.

Figure 61. On pointe in parallel.

Figure 62. Incorrect. Note the dancer is too far over the box and past the platform.

Figure 63. Incorrect. Note the dancer is not on top of the platform and is on the back of the box.

Chapter 4

Conditioning for Ballet

I've been using conditioning exercises at the beginning of ballet class for more than twenty years. Developing the correct muscles and muscle usage builds strong and healthy dancers. As I mentioned before, in America, among many other cultures, we train all types of bodies to dance. Thus, we encounter dancers who need instruction on how to turn out, hold their center properly, straighten their knees, and so forth. Regrettably, teachers frequently command "Pull up!" or "Turn out!" without clearly describing how to do so. Dancers then do their best but often execute turnout or movement incorrectly. At best, this leads to ugly lines. At worst, it leads to misalignment, weakness, and serious injuries.

Conditioning can help. Offer your students a wide variety of conditioning exercises to help them develop proper alignment, classical lines, and musculature. Include a few exercises at the beginning of class and explain exactly what purpose each exercise serves so that it relates to actual dance movement. The supplementary goal is for dancers to be able to feel the correct muscles to use during particular movements so they can use those same muscles when standing and carrying out the related ballet vocabulary. You must make that connection for them! Occasionally, put a conditioning exercise into the middle of class to prepare to work on a specific skill right before they practice that skill.

I recommend five to seven minutes on average per class spent on conditioning; however, you can periodically use a larger chunk of class time when your students will profit from a designated effort on a specific technical issue. You will not be able to fit all the exercises into a single class, but over time, you can teach your students each one. Pick the few that most benefit the group of dancers you have in front of you and insert them routinely into class. Tell your dancers these exercises are for their benefit. They should learn them and do them on their own time, since they'll get only a few minutes during class to practice. It's their responsibility to know what their bodies need and to spend daily time at home conditioning and stretching. Ingrain the idea that their lives are their own, and only they can do the work needed to become professional dancers. If they want it, they'll do the work outside of class.

In this chapter, I list technical and body-development areas that regular conditioning can help improve. Under each area, I offer several exercises with clarification and photographs featuring experienced students and professional dancers performing them.

Exercises for the Core, Center, and Abdominals

Leg Slide for the Center/Core

Use the abs and lower back to find one's center or core alignment and hold and shape the back.

This exercise is excellent for ages seven and up in parallel, and for ages nine and up turned out with both legs in retiré (what dancers call the "butterfly" position).

1. Lie on your back with both legs bent, parallel, feet on the floor and close to your body.

2. Tighten your abs, press your belly button through to the floor, and make sure your lower back and bottom are flat on the floor.

3. Your chest and shoulders should remain soft so you can breathe in and out easily.

4. Slide your feet along the floor, away from your tailbone, until your legs are halfway straight. You don't need to keep your feet flat on the floor.

5. You do need to keep your lower back on the floor by tightening your ab muscles toward the ground.

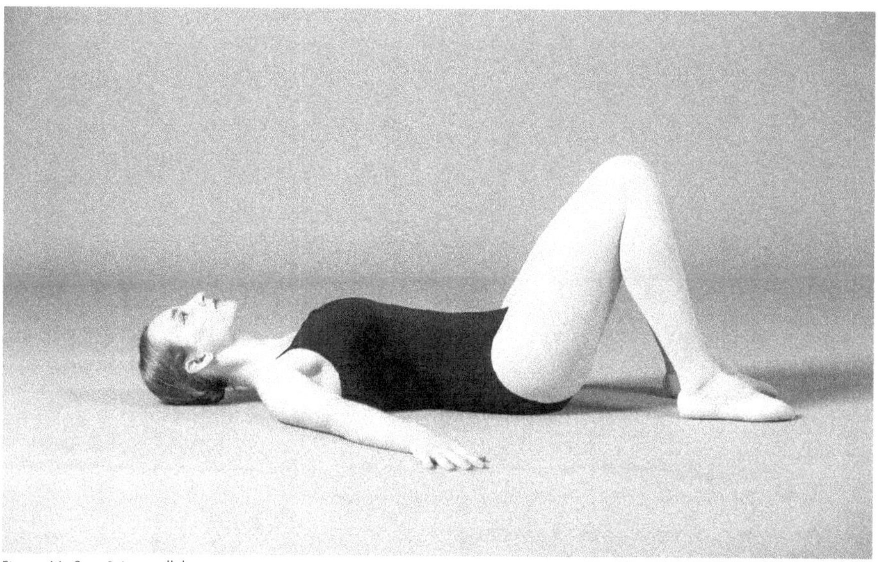

Figure 64. Step 1 In parallel.

6. Check often that you're still breathing easily and that your shoulders are relaxed and away from your ears. (Shoulders are not earrings.)

7. Hold this position for twenty to thirty seconds and notice what it feels like to maintain your abs and back this way. This is the sensation in your abs you need to feel for proper alignment or to hold your core in place while standing.

8. Do not attempt to straighten your legs all the way while keeping your back on the floor. This would create a tucked pelvis position, which isn't what we're looking for. You should only straighten your legs an inch or two past halfway, at most.

9. Hold this position for thirty seconds and then immediately stand up in parallel and try it. Practice standing in various positions and using the memory of how your abs and back felt on the floor to hold your center in alignment while standing.

10. Repeat the same exercise turning out. Begin by lying on your back with both legs in retiré, or butterfly position. Feet should point without sickling.

See Figure 64, Figure 65, Figure 66, Figure 67

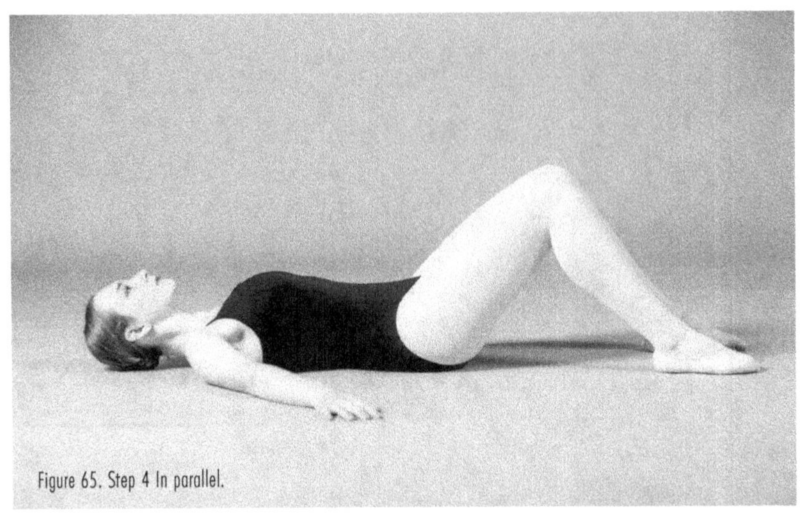

Figure 65. Step 4 In parallel.

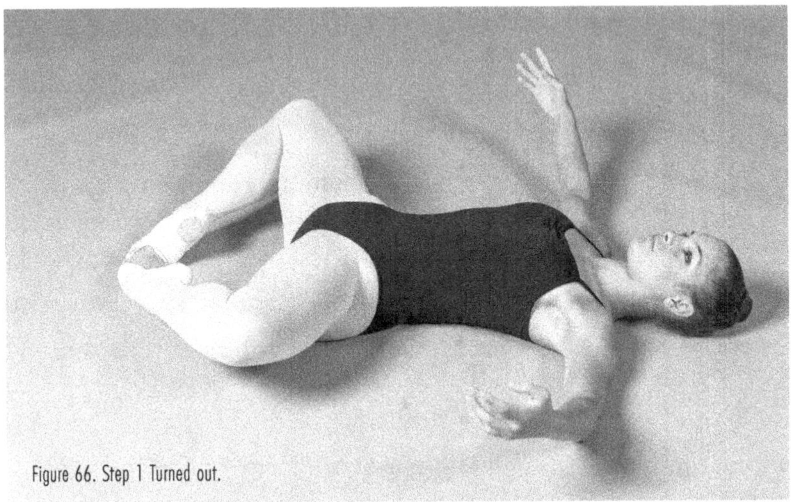

Figure 66. Step 1 Turned out.

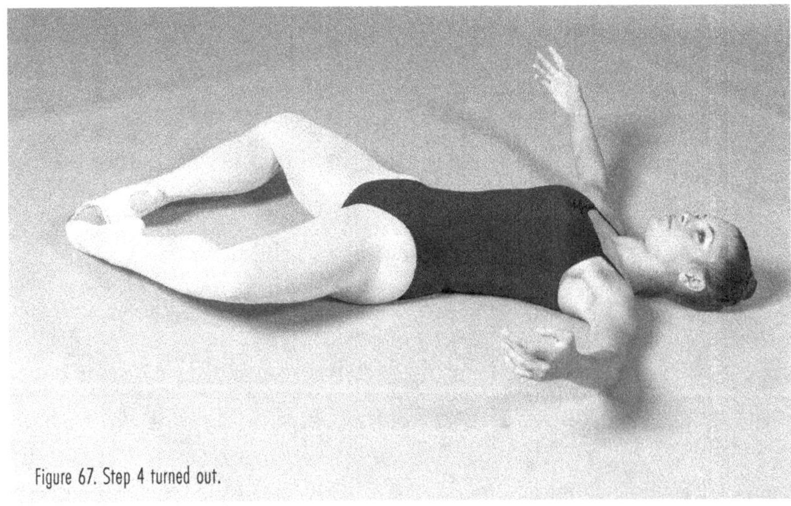

Figure 67. Step 4 turned out.

Curling and Rolling Abs for the Center/Core

Use abdominal muscles to find center and core alignment by aligning the back and hips.

This exercise can be taught by the age of nine or ten. Use your discretion based on the experience of the students in any given class.

1. Lie on your back with both legs bent, parallel, feet on the floor and comfortably close to your body, a little more than halfway bent.

Figure 68. Step 1 Hips and back flat on the floor.

2. Use only the abdominal muscles in this exercise. You'll be tempted to push your feet and legs into the floor and squeeze your bottom. Don't. Using additional body parts to do the work will fail to isolate the muscles needed.

3. The goal is to roll your hips as though they were a sleeping bag being rolled up. Use only your abs to roll your back and hips into a concave shape, in which your belly button is sinking into your back, like the shape of a smile or a lower case "u." You shouldn't in any way push your hips off the floor; that's a different exercise.

4. Next, unroll your hips all the way to the opposite shape—that of a rainbow—so your lower back actually comes off the floor.

5. Four counts to roll, four counts to unroll. Four to eight repetitions.

6. When you're standing, you should always be doing ten to fifteen percent of this rolled position, to hold your center or core in proper alignment. Doing more than ten to fifteen percent will cause your bottom to "tuck" under you, an undesired result.

See Figure 68, Figure 69, Figure 70

Figure 69. Step 3 Rolling the pelvis using only the abdominal muscles.

Figure 70. Step 4 The pelvis unrolled and released.

Circular Crunch for the Center/Core

Use the abs and turnout muscles to hold the hips in place and maintain turnout. While this exercise builds core control, it has the added bonus of opening the hips for turnout.

This exercise is intended for students at intermediate levels and higher.

1. Lie on the floor and place your legs into the butterfly position with both feet pointed, which means heels will be off the floor. Use your abs to keep your lower back pressed into the floor and open your knees to the floor during the entire exercise. Put your hands behind your head with elbows open to the side.

2. Lift your head and shoulders off the floor one inch while maintaining a space the size of an orange between your chin and chest. This will be known as the "back" position in this exercise.

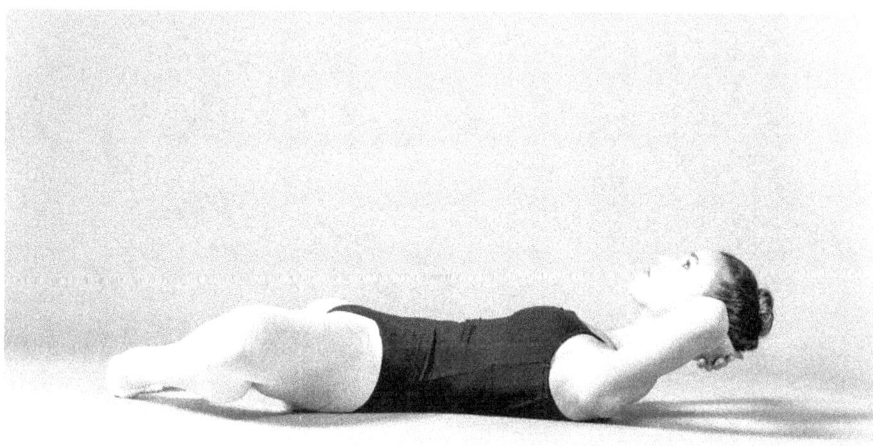

Figure 71. Step 2 Head and shoulders lift one inch.

3. Count 1: Lift higher and twist from your waist to the right. Count 2: Turn from your waist to the center. Count 3: Turn to the left. Count 4: Return to the "back" position. Keep your abs holding your lower back into the floor and continue opening your knees as close to the floor as possible throughout the exercise. Start with two sets right, two sets left, and repeat.

4. Work up to four sets right, four sets left, two sets right, two sets left, then single sets RLRLRLRL.

See Figure 71, Figure 72, Figure 73, Figure 74

Figure 72. Step 3 Lifted higher and twisted to the right.

Figure 73. Step 3 Returning to center, remaining lifted.

Figure 74. Step 3 Turning left from the waist.

Supporting-Side Core Control

Use the abs and core muscles to hold the supporting side in place.

This exercise is appropriate for ages nine and up. It teaches dancers to hold their supporting side still.

1. Begin lying on your back with both legs in parallel. Bend one leg so your foot rests on the floor and développé your other leg straight up in parallel or turned out.

2. Open the lifted leg to the side only as far as you can go without allowing any part of your back, ribs, hips, or bottom to twist off the floor. Hold your bent knee in parallel. Keep your arms soft so you're not relying on them to hold your body still.

Figure 75. Step 1 One leg bent with foot on the floor, one leg lifted.

Figure 76. Step 2 Lifted leg opens. Back and hips remain on the floor.

3. Return the open leg to a straight-up position by using the abs.

4. Counts 1 to 4: Open the leg. Counts 5 to 8: Return the leg upright. Four to eight repetitions.

See Figure 75, Figure 76

Exercises for the Hip Flexors

Knee Bends for Hip Flexor Lengthening, Lying on Stomach

This exercise is appropriate for students at an elementary level, ages ten and up. It teaches dancers to feel their hip flexors lengthened.

1. Lie on your stomach, forehead rested on your hands, legs in parallel with straight knees and relaxed or pointed feet.

2. Lengthen your hip flexors so the fronts and tops of your legs are completely flat on the floor, including the space between the tops of your thighs and the front of your hips. There should be no space between the floor and your body.

Figure 77. Step 2 Lengthen the hip flexors flat while lying on the stomach.

3. Bend your knees so your feet come up. Then straighten your knees, bringing your feet back down to the floor, all the while keeping the front of your legs, hips, and hip flexors touching the floor. This should cause no pain; however, it requires concentration in order not to release the front of your legs and hip flexors off the floor as you bend and straighten your knees. Pay attention to how it feels to keep your hip flexors along the floor as you move your legs. This lengthening is what you need to hold your pelvis in alignment when you're standing.

4. Counts 1 to 4: Bend. Counts 5 to 8: Straighten. Four to eight repetitions.

See Figure 77, Figure 78, Figure 79

Figure 78. Step 3 Begin to bend the knees. Keep the hip flexors long on the floor.

Figure 79. Step 3 Bend the knees all the way. Keep the hip flexors long on the floor.

Tucking Hip Flexor Stretch

This exercise is appropriate for students at a high elementary level and up. It lengthens and stretches the hip flexors.

1. Begin facing the barre and kneeling on your right knee in parallel. Left leg is in front and bent ninety degrees, foot flat on the floor. You can hold the barre.

2. Tuck your hips and pelvis under you and shift your weight onto your front left leg while maintaining your pelvic tuck. You should feel a stretch in the front of your right hip.

3. Hold for twenty to thirty seconds. Repeat other side.

See Figure 80, Figure 81

Figure 80. Step 2 Tuck the pelvis under.

Figure 81. Step 2 Transfer weight onto the front leg and maintain the pelvic tuck.

Bridge (Backbend) Stretch for Hip Flexors

This exercise is appropriate for students at an elementary level and up. It lengthens hip flexors.

1. Go into a "bridge" (backbend) from a sitting or standing position—however you prefer to get there.

2. Push your hip flexors high into the air instead of focusing on lifting your back and belly. Hold for ten seconds. Repeat once more. You may need to build up to the ten seconds over a period of a few weeks.

See Figure 82, Figure 83

Figure 82. Step 2 Lift the hip flexors high into the air.

Figure 83. Step 2 Incorrect. Note the hip flexors are relaxed down.

Exercises for Turnout and Rotation

Turning Out and Parallel Exercise for Turnout Strength

This exercise is appropriate for dancers at a primary level and up. I often have my students do this exercise first thing in class as a gentle way of "waking up" the turnout muscles. This exercise can be done sitting up or lying on the back with the legs straight up.

1. Sit up straight with your legs straight out in front of you in parallel and point your feet. Arms à la seconde.

2. Turn out your legs so that your knees face opposite walls in the room. Keep your legs straight and connected to each other the entire time. This

means that when you turn out, the backs of your legs will touch, and when you turn to parallel, the insides of your legs will touch. Hold.

Figure 84. Step 1 Legs in parallel.

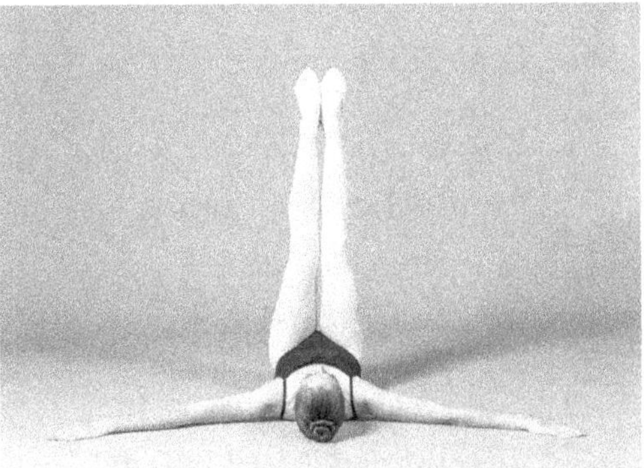

Figure 85. Step 1 Legs in parallel while lying on the back with legs lifted.

Figure 86. Step 1 Legs in parallel.

Figure 87. Step 2 Legs turned out.

3. Turn legs back to parallel.

4. Count 1: Turn out. Counts 2 to 3: Hold the turnout position. Count 4: Return to parallel. Complete four sets with pointed feet and four sets with flexed feet.

5. Turn out again with pointed feet and continue to turn out more and more for twenty to thirty seconds. Remember that turning out is a verb: it is something we do, not something static. The bones

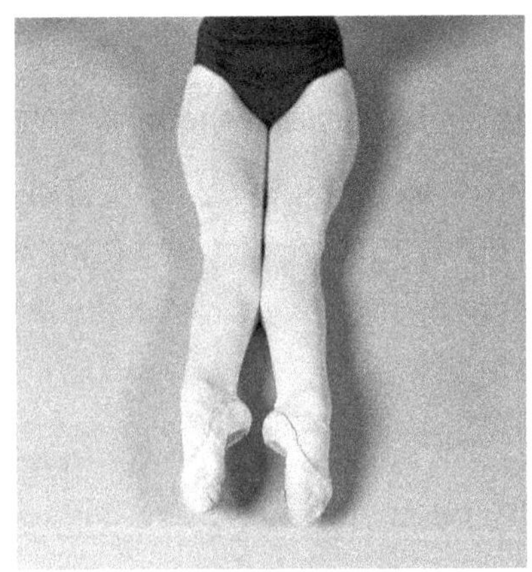

Figure 88. Step 2 Legs turned out.

inside your hip sockets actually turn in opposing directions, and your muscles turn the bones. Imagine your legs as two old barbershop poles—the ones with turning red and white stripes—touching each other and rotating away from each other. Continue to increase the amount of turnout until the time is up.

See Figure 84, Figure 85, Figure 86, Figure 87, Figure 88, Figure 89, Figure 90

Figure 89. Step 2 Legs turned out while lying on the back with legs lifted.

Figure 90. Step 2 Legs turned out.

Turnout Exercise Against the Wall

This exercise is appropriate for students ages nine and up. It teaches dancers to open their hips and legs while rotating. It can also be done in the center without a wall to support the dancer's back as long as the dancer is strong enough to hold their back straight on their own during the movement of the legs.

1. Sit on the floor with your back and hips against the wall to keep your back completely straight. Position your legs in butterfly with feet flexed and turned out, heels up, and toes flexed on the floor.

2. Straighten your legs while keeping your feet flexed, heels

Figure 91. Step 1 Legs in butterfly with feet flexed and heels lifted.

off the floor, and legs turned out as much as possible.

3. Point and flex your feet twice.

4. Bend your legs and feet back into the beginning position. Open the knees to the floor, lift the heels, and flex the toes down as you go.

Figure 92. Step 2 Begin to straighten the knees.

Figure 93. Step 2 Straighten the knees with feet flexed. Maintain the turnout.

Figure 94. Step 3 Point the feet. Maintain the turnout.

5. Counts 1 to 4: Straighten. Counts 5 to 8: Point and flex. Counts 1 to 4: Bend and open the knees. Counts 5 to 8: Hold your knees open to the floor as much as possible.

See Figure 91, Figure 92, Figure 93, Figure 94

Turning Out in Second on the Floor

This exercise is good for dancers ages eight and up, as long as they can sit on the floor with legs in second and keep their back straight.

1. Sit on the floor with your legs in second. This does not need to be a wide split. You should be in a position where you can sit straight with a neutral pelvis and maintain your balance upright without leaning forward.

2. Straighten your knees and flex your feet.

3. Turn your legs so your knees and tops of feet face behind you. Keep your knees straight. It will be tempting to lean forward. Monitor yourself and keep your back straight up and down as you turn your legs back.

4. Hold your knees facing back for ten seconds, then relax for ten seconds. Repeat three times. Then repeat with pointed feet.

See Figure 95, Figure 96

Figure 95. Step 3 Turn legs and knees to face the wall behind you.

Figure 96. Step 3 Turn legs and knees to face the wall behind you.

"Glued Feet" Turnout

This exercise is great for feeling turnout muscles and learning to turn out without forcing anything from the feet. Dancers ages eight and up will be able to do this exercise.

1. Stand facing the barre with both hands on the barre, feet in parallel, a few inches apart. Your heels should touch the floor, but you should not be leaning on your heels.

2. Imagine there is glue on the bottom of your shoes, and you can therefore not move your feet on the floor at all—not even a wiggle outward.

3. Now turn out your knees and thighs out past where your feet are facing while keeping your feet glued in parallel. Your legs won't turn far, but you will feel the motion of your muscles activating to turn out your legs. These turnout muscles should be engaged at all times while dancing.

4. Hold the legs turned out for ten seconds. Repeat three times.

5. Repeat in first position.

See Figure 97, Figure 98

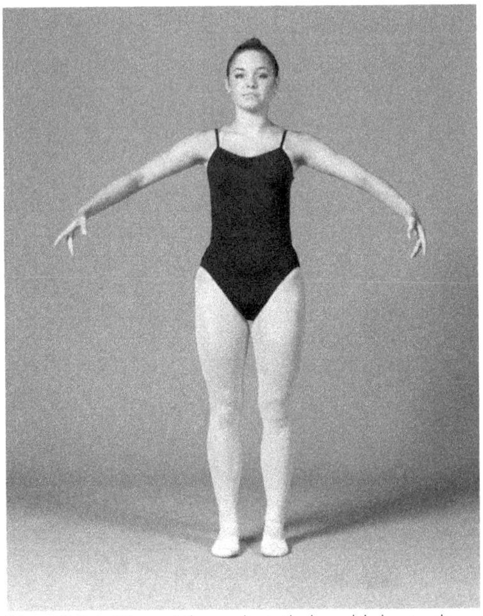

Figure 97. Step 1 Stand in parallel with relaxed leg muscles.

Figure 98. Step 3 Turn out the muscles in the legs while keeping the feet glued in place.

Note the subtle difference in the second photo—the dancer's knees in this photo are facing over her feet instead of slightly inwards. Because the movement is so small, you will need to look carefully to observe the modest difference in the direction of the dancer's knees, which indicates important muscle usage.

Pulsing on the Back

This exercise will build and strengthen the inner thigh and other turnout muscles. It's appropriate for dancers at an intermediate level and up.

1. Lie on your back, lift legs straight up, then open your legs to let them hang in second. Do not try to open your legs to the floor or stretch them far. Keep your lower back on the floor during this exercise.

2. While in the open position, straighten your knees, flex your feet, and turn out your legs. Your kneecaps and toes should face the floor, while your hamstrings, calves, and heels face the ceiling. This is the starting position. What you're feeling as you turn your kneecaps and quads to face the floor is the rotation of turning out. You should find this rotation sensation as you move your legs during the exercise.

Figure 99. Step 2 Turn out the legs while they are open in second.

3. Use eight counts to pulse your legs up and together into a first position. Each count is a slight pulsing motion, moving your legs a few inches higher and closer together toward first position. Continue to actively rotate your turnout the entire time while moving the legs up. Hold and turn out in first position. Then open your legs smoothly—without any pulsing to the starting position while still rotating your turnout. Rest.

Figure 100. Step 3 Pulse the legs up to first position. Maintain turnout.

4. Counts 1 to 8: Pulse up to first position. Counts 1 to 4: Hold first. Counts 5 to 8: Open smoothly back to the starting position.

5. Complete three repetitions with an eight-count rest in between each repetition.

See Figure 99, Figure 100, Figure 101

Figure 101. Step 3 Hold the turned-out first position.

Piriformis Stretches

The piriformis muscle operates the turning out of the hips. Overuse of the piriformis is common, and stretching it can be of great help to dancers. The following two stretches are appropriate for dancers eight and up.

1. Lie on your back with both legs bent in parallel and feet flat on the floor, hip distance apart. Cross your right ankle over your left knee, keeping your right knee open. Link your hands behind your left thigh and pull your left leg off the floor toward your chest. Be sure to keep your back on the floor. Hold for thirty to forty-five seconds. Repeat on other leg.

2. From a sitting or kneeling position, come forward and place both hands on the floor to a tabletop position. Bend the right knee, bring it forward, and turn it out so that the right knee is behind the right wrist, and the right ankle is behind the left wrist. Lengthen the left leg behind you

in parallel. This is what is also known as pigeon pose in yoga. Fold forward. Hold for twenty to thirty seconds. If folding all the way forward onto the floor is too intense, lean on your hands or elbows and keep your upper body off the floor.

Figure 102. Step 1 Lie on the back. Cross the right ankle over the left knee.

See Figure 102, Figure 103, Figure 104

Figure 103. Step 2 Bend one knee, turned out. Fold on top of it. Back leg is extended in parallel.

Figure 104. Step 2 Bend one knee, turned out. Fold on top of it. Back leg is extended in parallel.

Hip Joint Release

Dancers' hip joints often become overworked, strained, and tight from constant turnout work. This release is a great way to allow them to rest. Students of any age can handle this exercise.

1. Lie on your back with both legs bent in parallel and your feet flat on the floor, feet wider apart than hips.

2. Let your knees fall in toward each other. Do not push your knees together; wherever they fall naturally is fine. Some people's knees will touch, and others' will not. As long as you're allowing them to freely fall inward, you're correct. It is okay if the outside edges of your feet lift a little off the floor.

3. Hold for thirty to forty-five seconds. Do this release exercise after daily class or conditioning.

See Figure 105

Figure 105. Step 2 Let the knees fall in.

Exercises for the Knees and Backs of the Legs

Knee Exercise to Strengthen Lower Quads

Learning to straighten the knees involves strength and flexibility. This exercise strengthens the lower quads one must engage to have properly straight knees. It's appropriate for students at a high elementary level and up.

1. Sit with your back straight and legs straight out in front of you in parallel. You may find it helpful to sit against a wall to keep your back straight until you're strong enough to easily sit straight without support. Using the wall doesn't lessen this exercise's usefulness.

2. Tighten your right kneecap and lengthen your right leg while maintaining a parallel position and neither pointing nor flexing your right foot. Lift your right leg off the floor; it will not raise high. Hold for a count and then lower. Again, your back must remain straight and your hips must remain square with no turnout at all to isolate the lower quads.

3. Count 1: Tighten and lengthen. Count 2: Lift. Count 3: Hold. Count 4: Lower. To start, do four repetitions right, then four repetitions left. As you get stronger, you can add more repetitions and longer holds.

See Figure 106, Figure 107, Figure 108

Figure 106. Step 1 Legs in front in parallel.

Figure 107. Step 2 Lengthen and tighten the left kneecap.

Figure 108. Step 2 Lift only the left leg off the floor, keeping it straight and in parallel while the right leg remains on the ground.

Stretches for the Backs of the Legs

These two stretches help to straighten the knees by lengthening the muscles along the backs of the legs. The first stretch is appropriate for dancers at a primary level and up. The second is appropriate for dancers at an intermediate level and up.

1. Sit on your right knee with your left leg out in front of you in parallel and keep your right knee close to your left leg. Flex your left foot. Place your left hand next to you on the floor and reach your right hand over your flexed left foot, holding your toes. The eventual goal is to fold your body in half onto your left leg. Most dancers will not be able to do this. As long as you're reaching for your feet and holding where you can reach, you should feel a stretch along the back of your leg. Then turn out the left leg and repeat the stretch to feel the outer hamstring muscles. Repeat other side.

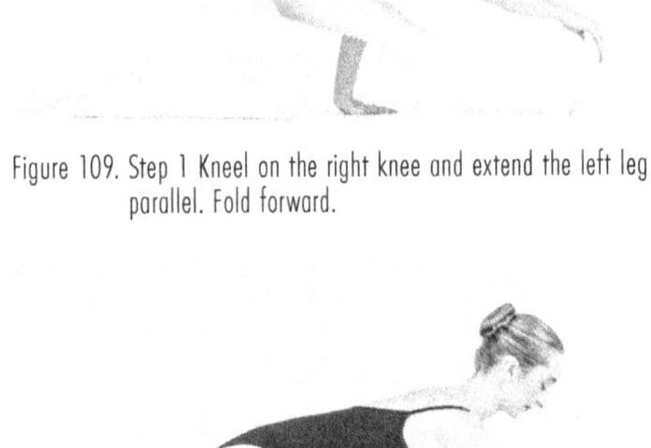

Figure 109. Step 1 Kneel on the right knee and extend the left leg in parallel. Fold forward.

Figure 110. Step 1 Turn out the left leg.

2. Stand and face the barre. Lift your right leg onto the barre with your foot flexed and your ankle resting on the barre in parallel, while standing on a partially turned-out left leg. Fold your right arm behind your back and reach your left arm forward to hold the flexed right foot. Keep your hips square and don't allow your right hip to inch forward. Hold for twenty to thirty seconds. Repeat other side.

See Figure 109, Figure 110, Figure 111

Figure 111. Step 2 Place the left leg on the barre in parallel. Fold forward.

Exercise to Straighten a Hyperextended Knee Correctly

This exercise is appropriate for dancers at an elementary level and up. It's important for dancers with hyperextended knees. Even if dancers don't have hyperextended knees, it can help train them to hold the lower quads and kneecaps to find a straight leg. Hyperextending the knees is acceptable and often desired in today's dance world for the working leg, as it creates a beautiful line, but no dancer should ever stand on a hyperextended knee. Unfortunately, many teachers will have students jam their heels together into first position in order to combat a hyperextended supporting leg, but that leaves dancers with bent knees and an unstable base on which to stand. This exercise teaches dancers what true straight is so they can stand on a straight and supported leg without hyperextending or bending the knee. It will give them a strong base to stand on.

1. Sit on the floor with your legs out in front of you in parallel.

Figure 112. Step 1 Legs in front in parallel with straight knees. Allow the heels to lift.

2. Point your feet, straighten your knees, and pull your kneecaps as tight as possible, while keeping your heels on the floor. If you have hyperextended legs, you'll feel as if they want to allow your heels off the floor, but doing so allows the knees to hyperextend. Try to straighten your legs as much as possible by pulling up the kneecaps—getting rid of the space underneath your knees between the backs of your knees and the floor— while keeping your heels on the floor.

Figure 113. Step 2 Keep the heels on the floor while straightening the knees.

3. The way the muscles in your knees and legs feel now with your heels on the floor is true straight: it's the feeling you should aim for when you're standing on your leg. A standing leg should never hyperextend. Try it out: stand up into first position immediately after doing this exercise. Make your knees feel exactly as they did when you were on the floor, keeping your heels down, but now stand in first position. You need not jam your heels into each other, but you should put your heels as close together as you can while maintaining what you've just learned to feel your legs in true straight.

See Figure 112, Figure 113

Exercises for the Feet

Foot Articulation

This exercise is appropriate for dancers at a primary level and up.

1. Sit on the floor with your legs out in front of you in parallel. Keep your knees straight. Start with feet, ankles, and toes pointed.

2. Part 1: Maintain the pointed stretch from your ankles while flexing and pointing your toes alone. Do this four to eight times.

3. Part 2: Flex both your ankles and toes. From here, maintain your flexed ankle while curling and flexing only your toes. Do this four to eight times.

4. Part 3: Keep your toes flexed while stretching and flexing from your ankles only. Do this four to eight times.

5. Part 4: Articulate through each part. Point your feet, point your toes, flex your toes, flex your feet. Do this section four to eight times as well.

See Figure 114, Figure 115, Figure 116, Figure 117

Figure 114. Step 1 Feet and toes pointed.

Figure 115. Step 2 Flex and point the toes only.

Figure 116. Step 3 Flex the feet and toes.

Figure 117. Step 3 Curl and flex the toes. Keep the ankle flexed.

Exercises for Jumping

Wall Exercise for Jumping

This exercise is appropriate for elementary levels and up. It teaches dancers to use their legs to push when jumping. It's crucial to have your dancers wear a shirt over their class uniforms so they don't get floor burns.

1. Lie on the floor with your feet flat against the wall and your knees bent at ninety degrees or less—whatever is comfortable for your knees. Your hands should be crossed on your chest or belly. Lift your head slightly off the floor and keep it lifted throughout the exercise.

2. Push as hard as you can off the wall, fully using your legs, feet, and toes. You will slide away from the wall, so you need to keep your head and feet off the floor as you slide.

Figure 118. Step 1 Knees bent. Feet against the wall.

3. Stand up right after doing this exercise so you can practice pushing away from the floor in jumps the same way you just pushed away from the wall.

See Figure 118, Figure 119

Figure 119. Step 2 Push off the wall. Keep the head, hands, and feet off the floor.

Exercises for Extension

Hip Range of Motion and Développés

This exercise is appropriate for dancers at an intermediate level and up. It helps dancers to feel mobility within the hip socket without compromising the alignment of their hips, to hold their supporting side, and to increase range of motion.

1. Begin on your back in the butterfly position, meaning both legs will be in retiré, feet pointed, and heels lifted. Press abs inward enough that your lower back is on the floor. Arms à la seconde.

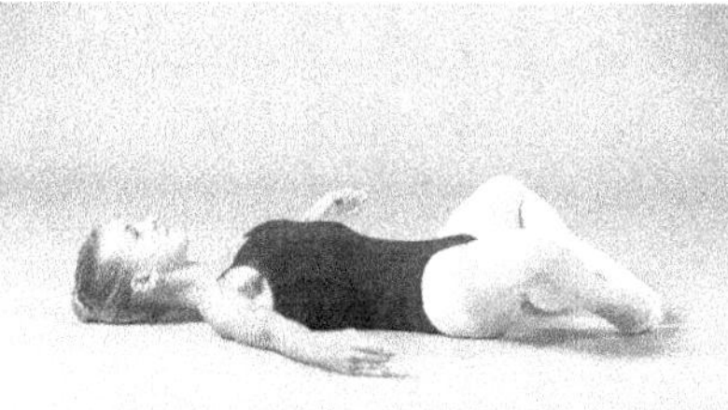

Figure 120. Step 1 Begin in butterfly.

2. Turn your right knee into parallel, only as far as you can turn it without disturbing the placement of the rest of your body. Your left leg remains turned out, and your lower back and both hips remain square on the floor.

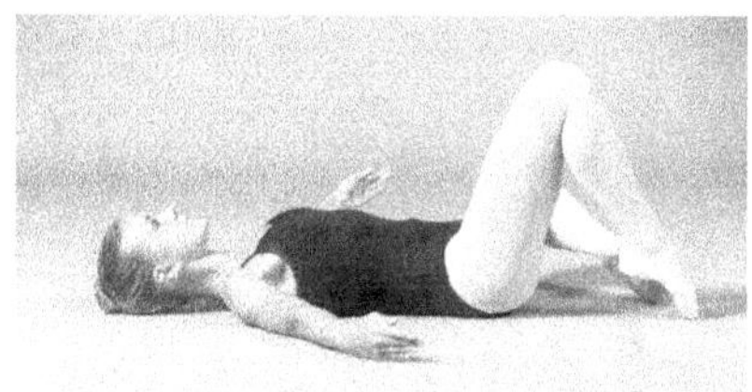

Figure 121. Step 2 Turn the right knee to parallel.

3. Pull your right knee back toward your chest while keeping it in parallel and also keeping your back and bottom squarely lengthened on the floor.

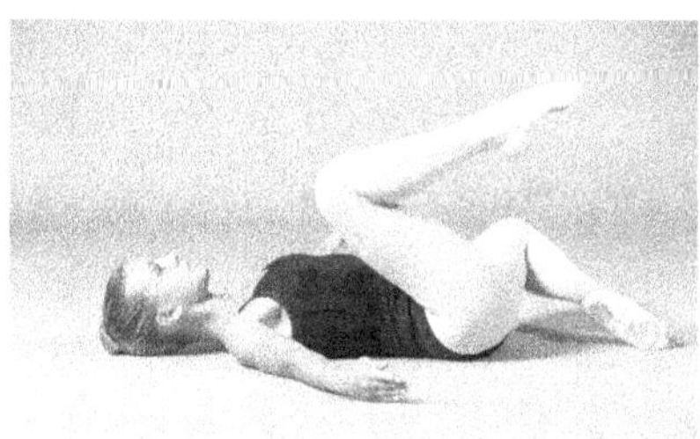

Figure 122. Step 3 Pull the right knee toward the chest. Keep the hips on the floor.

4. Turn out your right knee as far as you can while still bracing the left side of your body flat. Do not lift any weight off the left side of your body.

5. Lower the right foot back to the floor to the starting position.

6. Repeat four times on the right leg, four times on the left leg.

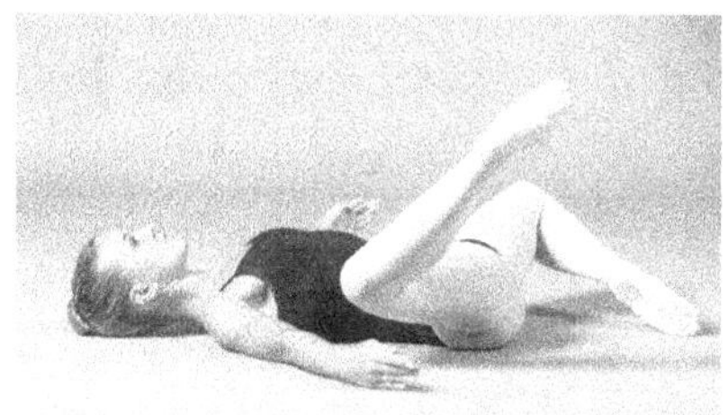

Figure 123. Step 4 Turn out the right knee. Keep the back flat and the left knee open.

See Figure 120, Figure 121, Figure 122, Figure 123

Développé Devant

This exercise is appropriate for dancers at an intermediate level and up.

1. Begin on your back with your legs in butterfly, meaning both legs will be in retiré, feet pointed, and heels lifted. Press abs inward enough that your lower back is on the floor. Arms à la seconde.

2. Bring the inside of your right ankle bone from the retiré position toward your chin in a similar fashion to attitude devant. Keep your back and hips squarely on the floor and your right knee open while the right ankle bone crosses directly in front of your chin.

3. Straighten your right leg so the inside of the right ankle bone still faces your chin and the little toes face away from the chin, as though you were completing a développé devant. It's important to keep the entire leg turned out. Both hips and back must remain squarely on the floor, which may inhibit how far you can lift the leg. That's fine.

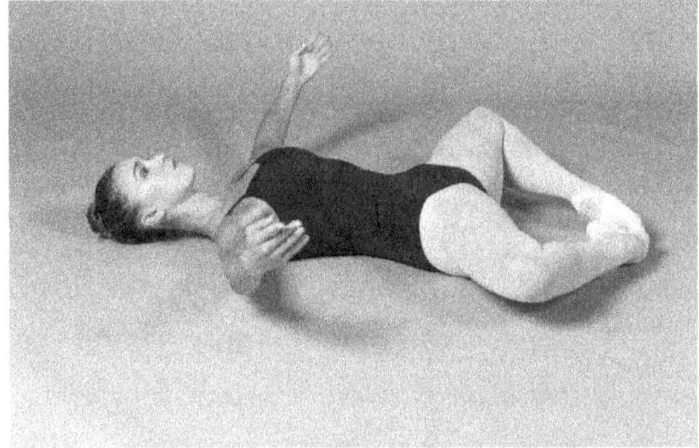

Figure 124. Step 1 Lie on the floor in butterfly, feet pointed.

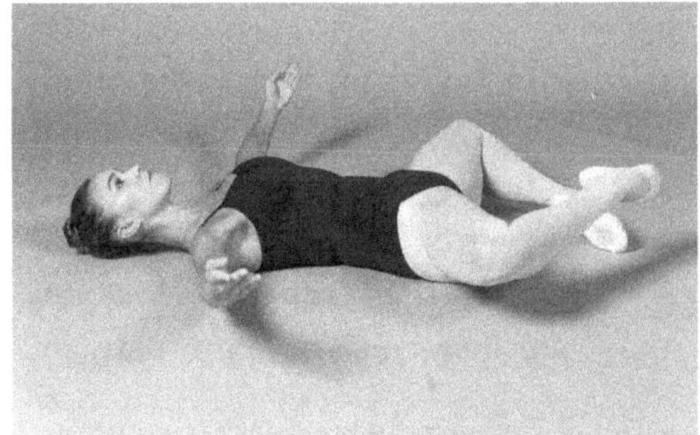

Figure 125. Step 2 Lift the right foot without lifting the right knee or moving the core.

Figure 126. Step 3 Straighten to développé devant keeping both hips on the floor.

4. Bend your right leg back into an attitude position, keeping the right knee turned out.

5. Return to the start position.

6. Counts 1 to 4: Lift into attitude. Counts 5 to 8: Straighten leg. Counts 1 to 4: Return to attitude. Counts 5 to 8: Return to start. Alternate right and left, completing two sets each.

See Figure 124, Figure 125, Figure 126

Développé à la Seconde

This exercise is appropriate for dancers at an intermediate level and up.

1. Begin on your back with your legs in butterfly, meaning both legs will be in retiré, feet pointed, and heels lifted. Press abs inward enough that your lower back is on the floor. Arms à la seconde.

2. Pull your right knee open and slightly up toward your right ear while keeping it as close to the floor as you can. The heel should be off the floor and turned out. Hold the left side of your body flat on the floor with the left knee open and your left hip still square on the floor.

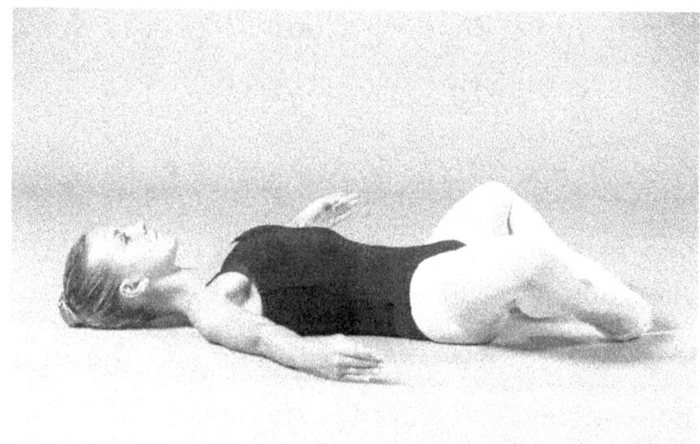

Figure 127. Step 1 Lie on the floor in butterfly, feet pointed.

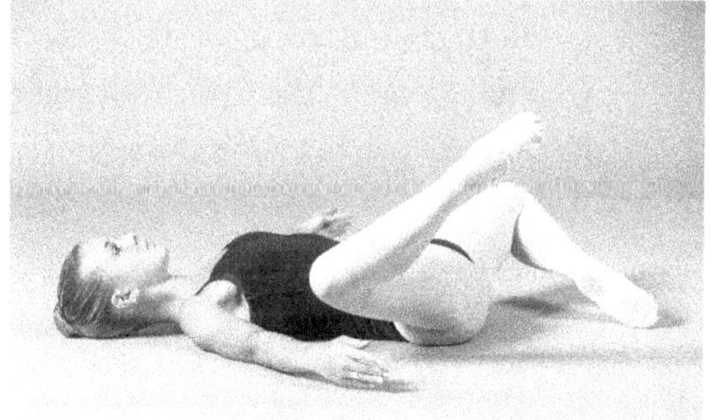

Figure 128. Step 2 Lift the right knee and open it. Keep both hips square on the floor.

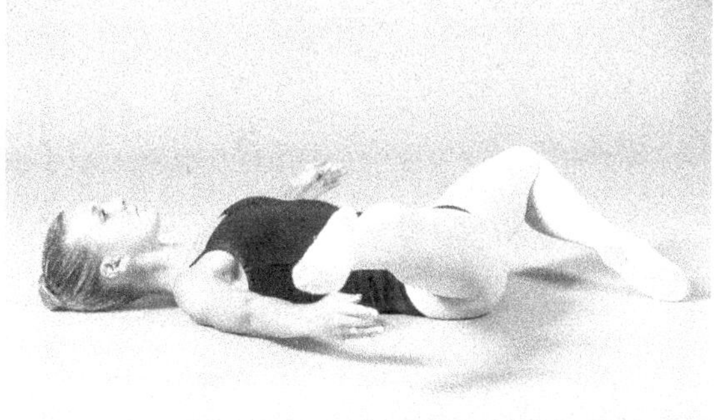

Figure 129. Step 3 Straighten the right leg to développé à la seconde.

3. Straighten your right leg to second, as though you were completing a développé à la seconde. You should feel the leg rotating so that your right knee is turning to face the floor. The entire time, hold your abs, back, and left hip flat on the floor and keep your left knee open.

4. Bend the right knee back to a retiré position, keeping your heel lifted.

5. Lower your right leg to the starting position.

6. Counts 1 to 4: Pull knee toward ear. Counts 5 to 8: Straighten leg. Counts 1 to 4: Bend leg. Counts 5 to 8: Lower leg to start. Alternate right and left, completing two sets each.

See Figure 127, Figure 128, Figure 129

Arabesque

This exercise teaches dancers to use the correct muscles to move the leg behind them without pushing the hips back or leaning back onto the heels.

The exercise is appropriate for dancers at an elementary level and up.

1. Lie on your stomach, upper back raised, supported on your elbows, with your hands flat on the floor. Your legs should be behind you in a pointed first position on the floor. Bring the legs to touch in first position as long

Figure 130. Step 1 Lie on the stomach, upper back raised, supported on the elbows. Both hips on the floor.

as it causes no strain on your lower back and as long as you can elongate both hip flexors on the floor the entire time, no matter which leg is being lifted. Your "supporting" leg and both hips should remain equally on the floor during the entire exercise. Keeping both hips grounded and square isolates the leg muscles needed in arabesque. When you stand up and do an actual arabesque with the leg lifted above 45 degrees, you should not keep your hips this square. This exercise serves to help you find the necessary leg muscles for lifting the leg into arabesque.

2. Lift your right leg, keeping both hips squarely on the floor. It will be tempting to lean or lift the right hip off the floor. Keep the leg straight and directly behind the shoulder. It may be hard to lift the leg while maintaining proper alignment—that's normal. It's fine to lift the leg only barely off the floor. Repeat to the left.

3. A more advanced version is to lift the arm of the working leg as you lift the leg.

4. Count 1: Lift the leg. Counts 2 to 7: Hold. Count 8: Lower. Repeat right and left, four to eight times.

See Figure 130, Figure 131

Figure 131. Step 2 Lift the left leg. Keep both hips fully on the floor.

Attitude Derrière and Développé Arabesque

This exercise is appropriate for dancers at an intermediate level and up.

1. Begin this exercise lying on your stomach with both legs turned out: right leg in retiré, left leg straight with a pointed foot. Both hips and both sets of hip flexors should be lengthened along the floor. If your right foot and ankle must remain off the floor for you to hold both hips on the floor, that's okay. Rest your forehead on your hands.

2. Lift your right knee off the floor. Both hips should remain pressed into the floor, and your right foot should not come any higher off the floor than it already was in your starting position. This will be difficult. You'll feel as if you need to lift your right foot in order to lift the knee at all. Don't. Your knee may barely move.

Figure 132. Step 1 Lie on the floor with one leg in retiré. Both hips on the floor.

Figure 133. Step 2 Lift the working (retiré) knee while keeping both hips square on the floor.

In fact, you may only be able to lift some weight off your right knee at first. Not a problem. This proper use of the muscles will help you feel the correct muscles to use in an attitude derrière. Be sure to keep the right side of the body elongated along the floor during the attempt to lift the right knee only. As long as you're keeping your torso, hips, and right foot down, the motion of lifting the right knee alone will help you feel how to lift your leg back into attitude and arabesque without squeezing the working side of the back.

3. Lower the knee.

4. Count 1: Lift the knee. Counts 2 to 7: Hold. Count 8: Lower. Do twice right, twice left.

See Figure 132, Figure 133

Exercises for the Arms and Shoulders

Stretching the Arms and Shoulders

This exercise is appropriate for dancers ages nine and up. It stretches the shoulders and arms.

1. Begin standing next to a wall, facing sideways. Lengthen your arm along the wall behind you, palm facing the wall, and keep your body close to the wall so that your arm is touching the wall as much as possible.

2. Hold for twenty to thirty seconds. Repeat other side.

See Figure 134

Figure 134. Step 1 Face sideways to the wall. Reach the arm back and hold.

Supported Elbows and Arms in Classical Positions

This exercise is appropriate for dancers at an elementary level and up. It teaches dancers to support their arms from their elbows, which engages the back. The feeling of holding the elbows while turning the hands back and keeping the shoulders down as they complete this exercise can be focused on and then translated into arms in second, first, and even fifth. You can sit or stand to do this exercise.

1. Extend both arms straight out to the side at shoulder height. Keep your shoulders down.

Figure 135. Step 1 Extend both arms at shoulder height. Keep the shoulders down.

2. Turn your arms forward from the shoulder so that the elbows end up on top and the palms face backward. Only turn as far as possible while

Figure 136. Step 2 Turn the arms forward from the shoulder joint to let the palms face behind you. Keep the shoulders down.

keeping your shoulders down. Turn your arms back to a normal amount of shoulder rotation.

3.   Repeat six to eight times.

4.   Turn your arms forward to the position with the elbows up and hold them there.

5.   Rotate your hands from the wrists back and open, then forward again. Hold the elbow up while turning the wrists back and forth.

Figure 137. Step 5 Rotate the wrist back and forward from the forward arm position.

6.   Repeat six to eight times. You can use the feeling of holding your muscles in this position with your arms turned forward and the hands turned back to understand the concept of supporting your arms from your back and elbows. From there you can work on creating the correct classical shapes while using your back and arm muscles. You should feel your back, shoulders, and arms working with this approach throughout your classical port de bras.

See Figure 135, Figure 136, Figure 137

Chapter 5

Level by Level

A ballet class level should include dancers who are close enough in ability and experience to be ready to work on the same concepts and classical steps. Dancers who are pushed or permitted to advance too quickly often miss learning fundamental technical elements that lead to weaknesses in their dancing.

Knowing how to separate students into levels can be challenging, but here's how I recommend thinking about it: Each level is a large, rectangular room with two doors, one on each end. Every room contains its own points of focus and goals—specific classical and musical concepts, and distinct movement vocabulary. Dancers start at a certain level when they're ready to begin addressing the steps and objectives within that room. They stay in the level for one to four years, until they've substantially mastered its objectives, at which point they leave that room and step through the door into another room with more advanced concepts and terminology to conquer.

In this chapter, I've arranged levels logically and listed concepts and steps that each level can work on—contingent upon the school operating a sound and professionally-oriented education program. The breadth and range of a school's syllabus would be different, smaller than what I offer here, in a recreational program where students attend class only one to three times per week. I want to underscore that any ballet students who attend fewer than the number of classes I suggest for each level in this chapter should be moving at a slower pace and addressing less vocabulary.

Stages such as Primary, Elementary, Intermediate, and Advanced should be divided into two or three individual levels in a curriculum. For example, where I have listed Elementary, you may have grades or levels Elementary 1 and Elementary 2 in your school. Your students spend one to two years in each of those grades. Not every grade will tackle every step listed; use your discretion based upon what the students in front of you need, how often they attend class, and how rigorous the training program is. Terminology named in each stage may not be addressed until students reach the later years of that level. The vocabulary and concepts listed in each level represent material students are able to begin working on during that level. Students should continue to improve and master those skills even as they advance through higher levels. Thus, the steps listed are steps to add to each level while students continue working on the steps and technical concepts from previous levels.

Please note that this book is not intended to be an unabridged book of pedagogy, so I have not listed every step within the ballet lexicon. What I have listed is a set of steps well suited, in a professional training environment, to the ages and levels named. In addition, I've not included a section on creative movement classes (ages three to four) or pre-ballet (ages five to seven) as many other useful books have been written on these subjects. See, for example, the works of Anne Green Gilbert and Mary Joyce. I will note that creative movement classes typically range from forty-five minutes to one hour, and pre-ballet classes should last one hour. The concepts covered in these classes focus less on technique and more on the rudiments of discipline, music, and movement; how to follow directions, stand in a straight line, and stand in a circle; the basics of counting both movement and music; and how to move quickly or slowly, lightly or heavily, sharply or smoothly, with the body high or low in space.

Ballet Fundamentals (7 to 8 Years Old)

Dancers at this level can think logically and follow directions for a full one-hour class that meets once or twice per week. They'll need one to three years at this level before they're ready to move on to the Primary levels.

Concepts to Cover

- Structure of a ballet class
- Etiquette in ballet class: hair, uniform, behavior

- Basic alignment
- Listening to the music as directions for dancing

At the Barre (facing the barre or away from the barre with the back facing the barre)

- Demi-plié
- Relevé
- Tendu
- Dégagé
- Rond de jambe à terre
- Grand battement

In the Center

- Tendu
- Relevé
- Positions of the feet (first, second, third)
- Positions of the arms (first, second, fifth)
- Temps lié

Across the Floor

- Walks on relevé, chassé
- Waltz step without turning (down, up, up)

Jumps

- Sauté (first and second)
- Échappé (from first and second)
- Changement (from third)

Thoughts and Helpful Hints

This level should line up outside the classroom and enter all together with a specific set of instructions about what to do upon entering. After reverence, they leave the classroom all together in a straight line as well. Do not dig deep anatomically into alignment at this level. An excellent way to teach them about their hips and pelvis at this age is to tell them to imagine their hips are a big bowl of cereal sitting atop their legs. They never want to spill cereal and milk all over the floor. It's a visual they can all relate to. Then, all you have to do is call out, "cereal bowls!" and they'll all straighten up to a good place.

Teach them about the history of ballet—how it comes from royalty—and remind them to dance with a crown on their heads. It's amazing how this helps them think about standing straight. At this level, all barre work should still be done facing the barre, with both hands on the barre, or occasionally facing away from the barre, with the back toward the barre and the elbows bent and both hands on the barre. If you have portable barres, turning them so the dancers can see you and themselves in the mirror is helpful at this level. Exercises should be done from first position. No fifth position yet. They can study third position of the feet as a pose to practice in itself. For jumps, make sure they understand the basic concept that every jump begins and ends with plié. No exceptions! You can tell them to push their feet and toes away from the floor to get into the air. For arms, suggest they imagine that their elbows are sitting atop a fluffy cloud when arms are in first or second, and they don't want to let their elbows sink into the cloud. These visuals allow the students to think about holding their bodies in a certain way without overwhelming them with anatomy and words they may not comprehend.

It's great at this level to give them three to four minutes of "free dance" time at the end of class. Play various styles and tempos of classical music and ask them to show with their bodies how the different pieces of music make them feel. Have them practice choosing an ending pose and holding it when you stop the music.

Primary Levels (8 to 10 Years Old)

Focus on mastering the basics of technique and classical vocabulary. Students will be ready to learn and perform numerous movements of ballet vocabulary on their own, but they won't be equipped to use the steps as part of combinations. Establish Primary 1 and Primary 2 levels, with the Primary 1 dancers being the less experienced, and begin work on the concepts and steps appropriate for each level. Dancers should attend at least two ballet classes per week when they're eight years old and three classes per week by the age of ten.

Concepts to Cover

- Everything from previous levels
- Alignment

- Distribution of weight on the feet
- Straightening knees without hyperextending
- Fifth position as a study (not to be used regularly in combinations)
- Support of the arms from the back and elbows
- Turnout
- Musicality in rhythm and quality of movement
- Sense of presence

At the Barre

- Everything from previous levels
- Pliés: demi in first, second, fifth and grand in first and second only
- Tendu: rolling through the foot heel, toe, toe, heel
- Dégagé
- Rond de jambe à terre
- Frappé
- Retiré (passé) as its own study
- Piqué
- Piqué pas de bourrée
- Développé
- Battement relevé lent
- Grand battement
- Pirouette preparation: practice snapping the heel and foot from fifth plié into retiré with a straight supporting knee; no relevé, no turn, facing the barre to start

In the Center

- Everything from previous levels
- Tendu
- Positions of the body: en face and croisé only
- First and second arabesque in tendu
- Relevé and sous-sus
- Pas de bourrée
- Balancé
- Pirouette preparation: practice snapping the heel and the foot from fifth plié into retiré with a straight supporting knee; no relevé, no turn

Across the Floor

- Everything from previous levels
- Waltz turn (in second or third year of Primary)
- Preparation for piqué turns
- Piqué turn
- Chassé

Jumps

- Everything from previous levels
- Changement
- Échappé sauté from first
- Assemblé
- Glissade
- Pas de chat
- Sissonne fermé en avant
- Chassé step temps levé
- Grand jeté

Thoughts and Helpful Hints

Use your judgment to determine what any particular class is ready to do. Students will be in a Primary level for one to three years. Dancers will not master most of the steps at this level, but they should have a clear understanding of their mechanics and the ability to execute them before moving on to the next level. The vocabulary for each step should be taught as its own study, not as part of larger combinations. Acquiring basic alignment, technique, and execution of the steps learned at this level is crucial to your students' future success. Even the most advanced, complex ballet steps begin with plié, tendu, or dégagé. Every single one! Take it slowly and allow your dancers to become proficient at individual steps.

Elementary Levels (9 to 12 Years Old)

Dancers in Elementary grades have the capacity to carry out foundational classical alignment and individual steps. They're ready to begin putting together simple, slow combinations with more than one or two elements. Establish both Elementary 1 and Elementary 2 levels, with the Elementary 1 dancers being less advanced. Elementary 1 dancers should attend class three times per week, and classes should be at least seventy-five minutes. Elementary 2 dancers should meet four times per week in classes of seventy-five or ninety minutes. Dancers in Elementary 2 will be ready to begin pointe work, fifteen to thirty minutes of which can be added to class two or three times per week.

Concepts to Cover

- Continuation of everything from previous levels
- Improving turnout as a verb: not something you have but something you do
- Strength
- En dehors and en dedans
- Improving extensions
- Improving flexibility
- Use of the head, arms, and upper body consistently with other movement
- Combinations with a few steps and elements put together
- Transitions, clean footwork in transition steps

At the Barre

- Everything from previous levels
- Fourth position as a study (no grand pliés in fourth)
- Grand plié in fifth
- Pas de cheval
- Sur-le-coup-de-pied: front, back, and wrapped
- Piqué
- Fondu: first as the practice of plié on one foot, later with fondu and extension
- Attitude devant and derrière
- Rond de jambe en l'air
- Grand rond de jambe en l'air
- Pirouette preparation: springing from fifth to retiré, begin turns at the teacher's discretion

In the Center

- Everything from previous levels
- Positions of the body: add effacé, écarté
- Tendu combinations with body positions
- First, second, third arabesque
- Pirouette preparation: spring to retiré with relevé, use quarter and half turns as well
- Pirouette: begin full turns as ready
- Piqué arabesque

Across the Floor

- Everything from previous levels with longer, more complex combinations
- Piqué turn en dedans
- Chaîné turns

Jumps

- Everything from previous levels
- Soubresaut
- Changement from fifth
- Royale (in last grade of Elementary)
- Sissonne simple
- Sissonne in multiple directions
- Échappé battu (in last grade of Elementary)
- Entrechat quatre
- Glissade
- Entrechat trois (later years of Elementary)
- Grands fouetté sauté (later years of Elementary)
- Grand jeté entrelacé (or tour jeté) (later years of Elementary)
- Grand jeté développé (or saut de chat)

Thoughts and Helpful Hints

Knowing your dancers and using your judgment is most crucial at this level and age group. Not all students will be ready for all the steps listed above. That's okay. Make sure your students get it right before moving on. Most important is that the dancers nail down their alignment, body positions, use of plié throughout movement, and control of the arms.

Intermediate Levels (11 to 16 Years Old)

Dancers at these levels are ready for moderately to considerably complex combinations. Include multiple steps, direction changes, transitions, and tempos. Students will still need balanced focus on basic technique but not as the singular focus of class. Again, establish two Intermediate classes: Intermediate 1 for the less-experienced students, and Intermediate 2 for students ready to work on more complex movement. Dancers should attend class a minimum of four times per week in the first year of an Intermediate level. By age fifteen, a serious ballet student will be in five or six ballet classes per week, along with additional pointe classes for women.

Concepts to Cover

- Continuation of everything from previous levels
- Long, complex combinations
- Long balances
- Multiple turns
- Connecting movement smoothly while completing every step and shape to its fullest
- Dynamics of movement and how it differs step to step

At the Barre

- Everything from previous levels
- Rond de jambe jeté
- Piqué fouetté

In the Center

- Everything from previous levels
- Penché
- Promenade en arabesque and in other positions
- Renversé

Across the Floor

- Everything from previous levels
- Emboîté turns
- Complex waltzes with multiple turns and direction changes

Jumps

- Everything from previous levels
- Entrechat cinq
- Assemblé battu
- Jeté battu
- Ballonné
- Ballotté
- Brisé
- Saut de basque
- Cabriole
- Temps de flèche
- Temps de cuisse

Thoughts and Helpful Hints

Schools often have one to three Intermediate levels within their program before dancers reach the Advanced level. Dancers begin their intermediate-level work still focused on technique, while also working on combining multiple steps, tempos, and directions into combinations. Over these few years, students will become adept at maintaining classical lines and a smooth, energetic sense of presentation while executing complex combinations. They need to remain in a high Intermediate-level class until they have mastered the blending of classical technique and quality of movement.

These years also coincide with changes in your students' personal lives as they pass through the sometimes tricky adolescent and teenage years. Preserve your ground rules and boundaries within the classroom. Although your students may feel frustrated with all the demands of ballet in the short term, they need your consistency and guidance to achieve success in the long term. They will come back and thank you later. That given, there are extenuating circumstances that create a need for compassion and some leniency. Use your judgment and be sure to define the terms when offering dancers any reprieve from the usual schedule or expectations about conduct.

Advanced Levels (14 to 20 Years Old)

Dancers at this level have mastered the necessary ballet technique required to execute the full classical vocabulary. They will still need to occasionally spend time reviewing and restrengthening particular techniques and muscles when obstacles arise. This level is the last before dancers move into a professional atmosphere as a trainee or a student at a college or university conservatory. Dancers in Advanced levels should be in ballet and pointe classes six days per week.

Concepts to Cover

- Continuation of everything from previous levels
- Learning long, complex combinations quickly
- Multiple tempos, direction changes, fast movement
- Artistry, storytelling, musicality
- Repertoire from classical ballets
- Most work on pointe for women

At the Barre

- Everything from previous levels

In the Center

- Everything from previous levels
- Multiple turns
- Fouetté turns

Across the Floor

- Everything from previous levels
- Multiple turns

Jumps

- Everything from previous levels
- Entrechat six for women, huite for men
- Brisé volé
- Gargouillade
- Revoltade (540) for men

Thoughts and Helpful Hints

Dancers will have learned most of the classical ballet vocabulary by the time they reach this level. The class pace should be quick, as little time is required to explain movement logistics, and dancers should not need to mark their exercises. Time should be spent using the vocabulary in more complex and long combinations, filling out music, and completing all movement. There should be a continued focus on the quality of movement and sense of presence.

A Note on Private Coaching and Lessons

Private lessons are popular today. Serious students and their dedicated parents often seek the personal attention of private coaching to achieve what they perceive to be the proverbial "leg up" on the competition. There is definitely a place for this. But private teaching cannot be the sole manner in which a dancer is educated. There are too many qualities essential to being a professional dancer that private work does not develop. These include working side by side with all types of personalities, following the rules and boundaries of a group, pushing oneself when one is not the star or center of attention, sharing space and traffic within classroom combinations and performances, and accepting awareness and responsibility for the group as a whole.

Specific situations do call for private instruction. Sometimes a student is alone in struggling with a distinct technical issue during class time. Arranging private lessons for a short period to help that student overcome that difficulty can be helpful. Some geographic areas will not have the quality of training needed locally. In that case, the young student should still attend classes locally a few times per week in the best school available to gain the experience of working in a group alongside instruction a few times per week with a professional coach, if the goal is to become a professional dancer.

Last, even within a professional training school, there are times when private coaching is worthwhile. Any student preparing for a solo role in a ballet performance or to compete in a ballet competition will need private coaching. This coaching will include work on storytelling, artistry and musicality, technical details, and polish.

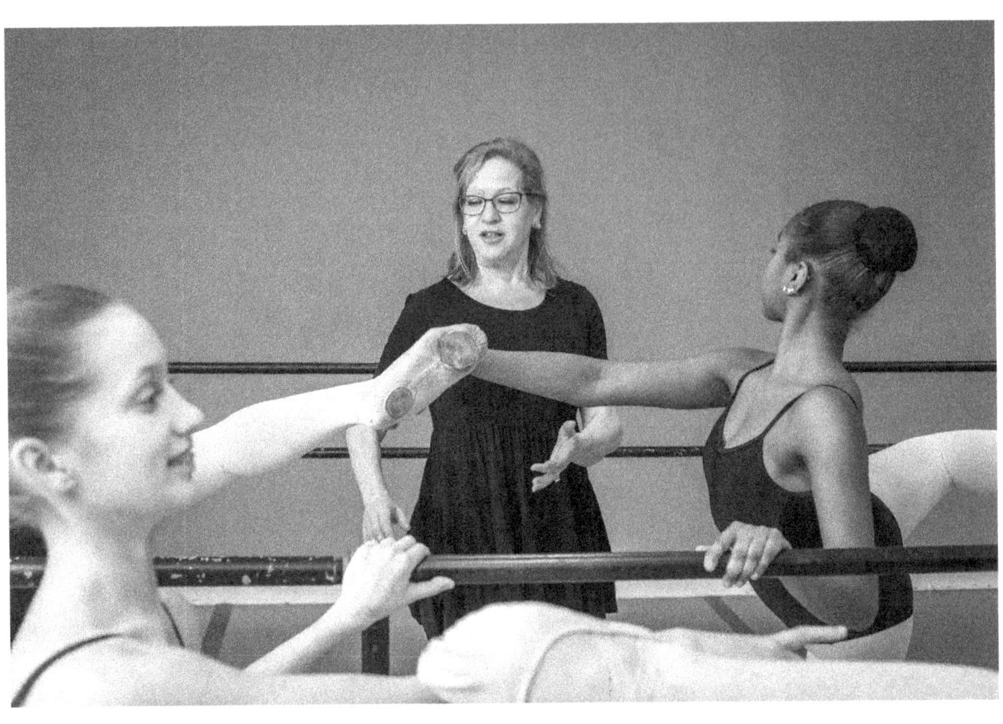

Chapter 6

Ballet Class Combinations

As a teacher, I appreciate learning about other instructors' class combinations to share them with my own students. In that spirit, I am sharing several combinations to give you an idea of the types of exercises appropriate for each level of experience, provided the students are following the professional training agenda I presented in the previous chapter, concerning the number of ballet classes per week and length of classes.

Primary Level Barre Work

1. Pliés at the barre

Start in first position facing the barre. Feet in first, arms in preparatory. Lift the arms to the barre to prepare. Adagio music.

Counts 1 to 12: Demi-plié in first position three times, bending for two counts and straightening for two counts each time.

Counts 13 to 16: Tendu à la seconde and lower the heel.

Repeat in second and third or fifth positions.

2. Cambrés at the barre

Start in first position facing the barre. Feet in first, arms in preparatory. Lift the arms to the barre to prepare.

Counts 1 to 4:	Turn head to the right.
Counts 5 to 8:	Cambré (bend) to the right from the waist. Keep legs and hips still.
Counts 1 to 4:	Straighten from the waist, still looking to the right.
Counts 5 to 8:	Turn head to the front.

Repeat to the left.

Counts 1 to 4:	Turn head to the right.
Counts 5 to 8:	Cambré back starting with the head and neck, without dropping the head back onto the neck and without bending any lower than the waist. Keep legs and hips still. Only bend as far as possible while keeping legs and hips in place.
Counts 1 to 4:	Straighten from the waist, still looking to the right.
Counts 5 to 8:	Turn head to the front.

Repeat to the left.

3. Tendus at the barre

Start in first position facing the barre. Feet in first, arms in preparatory. Lift the arms to the barre to prepare.

Counts 1 to 2:	Brush the right foot devant to the ball of the foot.
Counts 3 to 4:	Point the toes to complete the tendu.
Counts 5 to 6:	Lower the right toes to the floor, as in demi relevé.
Counts 7 to 8:	Close the foot into first position.

Repeat two more times devant.

Counts 1 to 4:	Élevé in first position.
Counts 5 to 8:	Lower back to first position.

Repeat en croix.

Demi-plié, relevé, balance in first position with arms off the barre in first position.

Repeat on the left.

4. Rond de jambe à terre at the barre

Start in first position facing the barre. Feet in first, arms in preparatory. Lift the arms to the barre to prepare.

Counts 1 to 12:   Three slow ronds de jambe à terre en dehors. Stop on each count in tendu front, side, back, and close.

Counts 13 to 16:   Demi-plié in first position.

Repeat en dedans.

Repeat on the left.

Once the dancers are strong enough, this exercise can be performed with one hand on the barre.

5. Grand battements at the barre

Start in first position facing away from the barre. Feet in first, arms in preparatory. Lift the arms through first into second, then hold the barre with the elbows bent in front of the barre to prepare.

Counts 1 to 4:   Tendu devant, grand battement up, lower to tendu, close first.

Repeat two more times devant.

Counts 13 to 16:   Bring arms off the barre into first and return them to the barre.

Repeat on the left. Then repeat right and left à la seconde.

Stop. Have the dancers turn to face the barre. Start in first position facing the barre. Feet in first, arms in preparatory. Lift the arms to the barre to prepare.

Counts 1 to 4:   Tendu derrière, grand battement behind the shoulder, lower to tendu, close first.

Repeat three more times on the right.

Repeat derrière with the left foot.

Primary Level Center Work

1. Tendus from first position

Start in first position en face. Arms in preparatory. Move the arms through first into second to prepare.

Counts 1 to 8:	Four tendus à la quatrième devant from first with the right foot.
Counts 1 to 4:	Demi-plié as arms close into first position.
Counts 5 to 8:	Straighten knees as arms open to second.

Repeat en croix.
Repeat on the left.

This exercise is appropriate for dancers in their first year or grade of Primary. In the second or third grade of Primary, this exercise can be done from third or fifth position.

2. Temps liés from first position

Start in first position en face. Arms in preparatory. Move the arms through first into second to prepare.

Count 1:	Tendu the right leg to the ball of the foot à la seconde.
Count 2:	Stretch the right toes to a full tendu à la seconde.
Count 3:	Lower the right toes to the floor, as in demi relevé.
Count 4:	Lower the right heel to the floor to second position.
Count 5:	Demi-plié in second position.
Count 6:	Push the left foot out of demi-plié into a tendu to the ball of the left foot in second.
Count 7:	Point the left toes to full tendu in second.
Count 8:	Close the left foot into first position.

Do this exercise right and left up to eight times.

As it is, this exercise is appropriate for dancers in their first year of Primary. In Primary 2, this exercise can be done from third or fifth position. It should then also be done into fourth position demi-plié with tendus front and back.

3. Sautés in first position

Start in first position en face. Arms in preparatory. Move the arms into first during the intro.

Counts 1 to 2:	Demi-plié in first position.
Count 3:	Sauté in first sur place.
Count 4:	Straighten knees.
Counts 5 to 8:	Repeat.
Counts 1 to 8:	Repeat the two sautés in first with the first jump traveling en avant (forward) and the second jump traveling en arrière (backward).
Counts 1 to 8:	Repeat the two sautés in first with the first jump traveling right and the second jump traveling left.
Counts 1 to 8:	Lift the arms through fifth, open them second, and close them back to preparatory.

If dancers are not ready to sauté and travel, this entire exercise can be done sur place.

Primary/Elementary Level Work

Here are exercises appropriate for dancers who have already spent one to two years in a Primary level, attend at least two classes per week, and are nearly ready to move into the Elementary level.

1. Rond de jambe à terre at the barre

Start in first position left side to the barre. Feet in first, arms in preparatory. Lift the arms through first into second to prepare. Take the barre with the left hand.

Counts 1 to 2:	Tendu the right foot devant and carry it to tendu à la seconde.
Count 3:	Hold.
Count 4:	Close into first.
Counts 5 to 6:	Tendu the right foot à la seconde and carry it back into tendu arabesque.
Count 7:	Hold.
Count 8:	Close into first.

Repeat two more times en dehors.

Counts 1 to 8:   Trace two slow, smooth ronds de jambe à terre en dehors.
Repeat en dedans.
Repeat on the left side en dehors and en dedans.

2. Tendus in croisé from third or fifth position in the center

Start in third or fifth position croisé with the right foot front. Arms in preparatory. Move the arms through first into a croisé arm with the right arm à la seconde and the left arm in fifth to prepare.

Counts 1 to 8:   Four tendus à la quatrième devant with the right foot.

Counts 1 to 4:   Demi-plié as arms close into first position.
Counts 5 to 8:   Straighten the knees as arms open to écarté, with the right arm high or low.

Counts 1 to 8:   Four tendus à la seconde in écarté, closing front, back, front, back.

Counts 1 to 8:   Plié and straighten as the arms close through first, then lift the right arm to fifth and the left arm to second.
Repeat this set derrière and then in écarté again so that you do it en croix.
Repeat on the left.

3. Changement in fifth position

Start in fifth position right foot front en face. Arms in preparatory. Arms lift to first to prepare.

Counts 1 to 2:   Plié.
Count 3:   Changement.
Count 4:   Straighten knees.
Counts 5 to 12:   Repeat two more times.
Counts 13 to 16:   Sous-sus and hold. Hands to the hips. Then plié and bring arms back to a preparatory position.
Repeat beginning with the left foot front.

Once dancers are in an Elementary level, this exercise can be done using croisé.

Elementary Level Barre Work

1. Tendus from first position

Start in first position left side to the barre. Arms in preparatory. Lift the arms through first into second to prepare. Take the barre with the left hand.

Counts 1 to 8: Tendu devant from first to the ball of the foot, point the toes, flex just the toes, flex the whole foot, point the foot without pointing the toes, point the toes to the floor, lower the toes to the ball of the foot, close first. Each of these movements is one of the eight counts of this phrase.

Counts 1 to 8: Two tendus devant, closing each in first. Out for two and close for two.

Complete this exercise en croix from first.

Repeat on the left.

The second set of eight counts in each position can be executed faster, with four tendus instead of two if the dancers are more experienced.

2. Tendus from fifth position

Start in fifth position right foot front, left side to the barre. Arms in preparatory. Lift the arms through first into second to prepare. Take the barre with the left hand.

Count 1: Slide the right foot from fifth directly into first. Remind the dancers to keep their little toes back.

Count 2: Tendu the right leg à la seconde.

Count 3: Close the right foot into first position.

Count 4: Slide the right foot from first directly into fifth position back.

Counts 5 to 8: Repeat en dedans.

Repeat en dehors and en dedans.

Counts 1 to 6: Tendu and close à la quatrième devant three times.

Counts 7 to 8: Tendu à la seconde and close fifth in back.

Counts 1 to 6: Tendu and close à la quatrième derrière (to arabesque) three times.

Counts 7 to 8: Tendu à la seconde and close fifth in front.

Repeat on the left.

3. Dégagé from fifth position

Start in fifth position right foot front, left side to the barre. Arms in preparatory. Lift the arms through first into second to prepare. Take the barre with the left hand.

Count 1:	Dégagé the right foot à la quatrième devant.
Counts 2 to 3:	Hold.
Count 4:	Close fifth devant.
Counts 5 to 8:	Repeat.
Counts 1 to 8:	Dégagé out à la quatrième devant. Close fifth front. Repeat three more times, out one count, close one count.
Counts 1 to 8:	Dégagé à la quatrième devant eight times, accent in to close on each count.
Count 1:	Dégagé out à la quatrième devant.
Counts 2 to 3:	Piqué two times.
Count 4:	Close fifth devant.
Counts 5 to 8:	Demi-plié and straighten.

Repeat en croix.
Repeat on the left.

4. Développés from fifth position

Start in fifth position right foot front, left side to the barre. Arms in preparatory. Lift the arms through first into second, and take the barre with the left hand to prepare.

Count 1:	Wrap the right foot sur le coup-de-pied and bring the right arm to preparatory.
Count 2:	Right foot to retiré devant and right arm to first.
Count 3:	Right leg to attitude devant and right arm to fifth.
Count 4:	Straighten the right leg to développé.
Counts 5 to 6:	Hold.
Count 7:	Lower the right leg to tendu devant.
Count 8:	Close the right leg into fifth and open the right arm à la seconde.

Complete the développés en croix, opening the arm in its appropriate positions.
Repeat on the left.

Elementary Level Center Work

1. Dégagé and sous-sus

Begin in fifth position with the right foot front en face. Arms in preparatory. Lift the arms through first into second to prepare.

Counts 1 to 2:	Demi-plié closing the arms into first.
Counts 3 to 4:	Straighten the knees and leave the arms in first.
Counts 5 to 6:	Demi-plié holding the arms in first.
Counts 7 to 8:	Sous-sus and bring the arms to fifth on 7. Hold 8.
Counts 1 to 8:	Hold the sous-sus position.
Counts 1 to 2:	Demi-plié and lower arms into first.
Counts 3 to 4:	Straighten the knees and open the arms à la seconde.
Counts 5 to 8:	Dégagé the right leg à la quatrième devant and close fifth two times.
Counts 1 to 4:	Two dégagés in second closing front then back.
Counts 5 to 8:	Two dégagés derrière to arabesque.

Repeat on the left.

Once dancers have completed a full year of Elementary work and are in their second or third Elementary grade, this exercise can be made more challenging. For example, within the eight-count sous-sus, the front leg can lift and coupé devant on Count 5 and return to sous-sus on Count 6. Then coupé the back leg and close sous-sus on Counts 7 and 8. The dégagés can also be faster: dancers would complete four dégagés front, second, and back, instead of two in each direction.

2. Temps lié

Begin in fifth position with the right foot front en face. Arms in preparatory. Lift the arms through first into second to prepare.

Counts 1 to 2:	Demi-plié. Lower the arms to preparatory.
Counts 3 to 4:	Tendu the right foot à la quatrième devant while still in plié on the left and bring the arms into first.

Counts 5 to 6:	Temps lié onto a straight right leg by pushing off the plié and transferring weight onto the right foot. The left foot is now in tendu derrière. The arms remain in first.
Counts 7 to 8:	Hold the tendu.
Counts 1 to 2:	Lift the left leg back to 45 degrees in arabesque.
Counts 3 to 4:	Lower the left leg to tendu back and close fifth.
Counts 5 to 8:	Port de bras bringing arms from first through fifth and opening second.

Repeat à la seconde. The left leg will close devant at the end so the exercise can be done devant and à la seconde on the left side.

This entire exercise can also be reversed so that it is executed derrière and à la seconde. Once dancers have completed a full year of Elementary work and are in their second or third Elementary grade, this exercise can be done using croisé and écarté arm and body positions.

3. Pirouettes

Begin in fifth position with the right foot front en face. Arms in preparatory. Lift the arms through first into second to prepare.

Count 1:	Tendu the right leg à la seconde.
Count 2:	Close the right foot into fifth position front in plié. Bring the right arm to first.
Count 3:	Retiré the right foot devant. Straighten the left leg without relevé. Both arms to first.
Count 4:	Close the right foot front into fifth position plié. Leave the arms in first.
Counts 5 to 8:	Repeat.

Repeat Counts 1 to 8 with a relevé.
Repeat again with half pirouettes.
Repeat again with single pirouettes.
Repeat on the left.

This exercise can be used in more advanced levels by adding multiple pirouettes instead of partial and single pirouettes.

4. Petit/medium allegro

Begin in fifth position with the left foot front en face. Arms in preparatory. Lift the arms through first into second to prepare.

Count 1:	Plié.
Count 2:	Hold.
Count 3:	Glissade to the right. Arms stay in second.
Count 4:	Straighten the knees.
Count 5:	Plié. Right arm closes to first, head turns to the right.
Count 6:	Hold.
Count 7:	Pas de chat to the right.
Count 8:	Straighten the knees.

Count 1:	Plié. Arms open to second, head turns front.
Count 2:	Hold.
Count 3:	Glissade to the right.
Count 4:	Pas de chat to the right. Right arms closes first, and head turns to the right.
Count 5:	Assemblé dessus (over). Arms open to second, and head turns front.
Count 6:	Sous-sus.
Count 7:	Hold.
Count 8:	Hold.

Repeat on the left.

Exercises for Elementary/Intermediate (Advanced Elementary)

These exercises are appropriate for dancers who have already spent one to two years in an Elementary grade, attend at least three classes per week, and are nearly ready to move into the Intermediate level.

1. Waltz with pirouettes

Begin in "B plus" position, which is attitude à terre, with the left foot front en face. Arms in preparatory. Lift the arms through first into second to prepare.

Counts 1 to 2:	Balancé right and left. The left arm closes first and then the right arm.
Counts & 3:	Piqué to the right, closing the left foot front in sous-sus into a soutenu turn to the right. Arms close fifth through first.
Count 4:	Retiré the right foot devant staying in relevé. Arms remain in fifth.
Count &:	Close the right foot back into fourth position demi-plié in croisé. Arms prepare for pirouettes.
Count 5:	Pirouette en dehors.
Counts 6 to 7:	Right foot down in fourth back croisé with the left knee bent. Hold pose.
Count 8:	Tendu the right foot back.

Repeat two more times.

Counts 1 to 2:	Fouetté in tendu, turning to the right so the right foot ends up tendu croisé devant. The left arm lifts to fifth, and the right arm opens second into croisé arms.
Counts 3 to 4:	Tombé onto the right foot. Prepare for pirouette en dedans.
Counts 5 to 6:	Pirouette en dedans, turning to the right. Arms close to first or fifth.
Counts 7 to 8:	Close the left foot front into fifth plié.

Repeat on the left.

2. Grand allegro

This exercise travels across the floor from the corner. Begin in B plus with left foot front croisé, in the upstage left corner. Arms in preparatory. Lift the arms through first into second to prepare.

Count 1:	Chassé devant with the right foot toward the downstage right corner. Arms close into first.
Count 2:	Temps levé on the right foot in second arabesque (sauté arabesque).
Count 3:	Chassé with the left foot. Arms close into first.
Count 4:	Temps levé on the left foot in second arabesque (sauté arabesque).
Count 5:	Run right left. Close the arms into first.
Count 6:	Grand jeté with the right leg. Arms to second arabesque.
Count 7:	Tombé on the left foot.
Count 8:	Piqué right then left into a sous-sus pose, bringing the left foot front into sous-sus in croisé. Arms go to fifth.

Repeat on the left.

Beginner Pointe Work for Elementary 2

In their second, third, or fourth year of Elementary studies, dancers are ready to begin pointe work. They should have established a sound basic technique with correct alignment of the core, strong knees, and strong feet and ankles. They should be in ballet class a minimum of three days per week before beginning pointe work.

1. Rolling up and down slowly at the barre

Begin facing the barre with both feet in parallel, a few inches apart from each other. Arms prepare to the barre.

Counts 1 to 4:	Roll up through the shoes onto full pointe.
Counts 5 to 8:	Hold.
Counts 1 to 8:	Roll down to flat using all eight counts.

Repeat this exercise twice in parallel and twice in first position.

2. Sous-sus

Start in fifth position right foot front, left side to the barre. Arms in preparatory. Lift the arms through first into second and take the barre with the left hand to prepare.

Counts 1 to 2:   Sous-sus and hold.
Counts 3 to 4:   Plié in fifth and hold.
Repeat six more sous-sus in this timing.
Counts 5 to 8:   Soutenu turn to the other side.
Repeat on the left.

3. Relevés on pointe in the center

Begin in first position en face. Arms prepare to first and remain there. Plié on the preparation.

Counts 1 to 4:   Relevé plié two times.
Count 5:   Relevé up.
Counts 6 to 7:   Hold.
Count 8:   Plié.

Perform this exercise four times while rolling up and down, and repeat it another four times springing up and down.

Intermediate Level Barre Work

1. Tendus from fifth position

Start in fifth position right foot front, left side to the barre. Arms in preparatory. Lift the arms through first into second and take the barre with the left hand to prepare.

Counts 1 to 2:   Two tendus à la quatrième devant closing fifth.
Counts 3 to 4:   Two tendus à la seconde closing fifth front then back.
Counts 5 to 6:   Two tendus derrière closing fifth.
Counts 7 to 8:   Chassé en avant (forward) with inside left foot to tendu the right foot back.
Counts 1 to 2:   Rond de jambe à terre en dedans with the right foot.

Counts 3 to 4:   Rond de jambe à terre en dehors with the right foot.

Counts & 5:   Close fifth back in plié and relevé on the left foot to coupé the right foot derrière.

Counts & 6:   Lower the left heel and développé (low) the right leg to tendu in second.

Counts & 7:   Coupé the right foot derrière and close it fifth in back.

Counts 8:   Hold.

Repeat en dedans.

Counts 1 to 16:   Sous-sus and cambré with port de bras forward and back.

Counts 1 to 16:   Balance of your choice.

2. Frappés and piqués

Start in fifth position right foot front, left side to the barre, arms in preparatory. Lift the arms through first into second and take the barre with the left hand to prepare on Counts 5 and 6. Then tendu the right foot à la seconde and bring it in flexed in preparation for frappé devant on Counts 7 and 8.

Counts 1 to 2:   Two frappés à la quatrième devant from a flexed foot.

Counts & 3:   Double frappé à la seconde, leaving the leg out.

Counts & 4:   Piqué in second, accent up.

Counts 5 to 8:   Four piqués, one in each direction en croix en dedans.

Repeat en dedans.

Counts 1 to 4:   Four double frappés à la seconde.

Counts 5 to 6:   Double frappé devant and then derrière.

Count 7:   Close the right foot fifth back in plié.

Count &:   Full soutenu turn détourné away from the barre.

Count 8:   Dégagé the right foot à la seconde while still in relevé.

Counts 1 to 2:   Hold.

Count 3:   Wrap the right foot sur le coup-de-pied.

Count 4:   Hold.

Counts & 5 to 7 &:   Battements sur le coup-de-pied ending back.

Count 8:   Lower the left heel and flex the right foot.

Repeat en dedans.

Repeat on the left.

3. Adagio for barre

Start in fifth position right foot front, left side to the barre. Arms in preparatory. Lift the arms through first into second and take the barre with the left hand to prepare.

Counts 1 to 2:	Développé the right foot devant bringing the right arm through preparatory and first into second. Plié on the left leg as the right leg straightens to développé.
Count 3:	Piqué en avant onto the right leg bringing the left leg to attitude derrière. The right arm lifts to fifth.
Count 4:	Hold.
Counts 5 to 7:	Plié and extend the left leg back into arabesque. Open the right arm second.
Count 8:	Close the left foot back into fifth as the right leg straightens.

Repeat with the inside leg and piqué back onto the left leg bringing the right leg to attitude devant.

Counts 1 to 4:	Développé the right leg à la seconde. Port de bras the right arm into second.
Counts 5 to 6:	Demi-rond the right leg to the front and plié on the left leg.
Counts & 7:	Relevé and fouetté en dedans and toward the barre, ending on relevé with the right leg in arabesque, the right arm on the barre, and the left arm second.
Count 8:	Hold.
Counts 1 to 2:	Brush the right leg through first into a slow battement devant at 90 degrees with the left leg in plié.
Counts & 3:	Relevé and fouetté en dedans and away from the barre, ending on relevé with the right leg in arabesque, left arm on the barre, right arm second.
Count 4:	Hold.
Count 5:	Retiré the right foot derrière. Bring both arms to first.
Counts 6 to 7:	Balance in retiré.
Count 8:	Close the right foot front into fifth position plié.

Repeat on the left.

Intermediate Level Center Work

1. Adagio

Begin in fifth position with the right foot front croisé. Arms in preparatory. Allow both arms to breathe open and then back to preparatory to prepare.

Counts 1 to 4:	Lift the right arm to fifth through second, and then do the same with the left arm.
Counts 5 to 6:	Chassé en avant lifting left leg into third arabesque. Arms go through first into third arabesque.
Count 7:	Hold third arabesque.
Count 8:	Close the left foot back in fifth. Arms open second and lower to preparatory.
Counts 1 to 2:	Développé the right leg à la quatrième devant. The arms open to croisé through first.
Counts 3 to 4:	Carry the leg and arms into second écarté devant, beginning a slow grand rond de jambe en l'air.
Counts 5 to 6:	Carry the leg and arms into first arabesque effacé, continuing the grand rond de jambe en l'air and lifting the left heel to turn to effacé.
Count 7:	Coupé the right foot derrière with a plié on the left leg. Arms close into first.
Count 8:	Quick pas de bourrée ending en face with right foot front in fifth.
Counts 1 to 4:	Développé right leg à la seconde and close back on Count 4.
Counts 5 to 7:	Développé the left leg à la seconde.
Counts & 8:	Close the left coupé derrière and pas de bourrée into fourth position left foot front croisé to prepare for pirouettes.
Counts 1 to 2:	Pirouette en dehors to the right.
Count 3:	Finish pirouettes in a plié on the left leg with the right leg in attitude derrière croisé.
Counts 4 to 6:	Hold.
Count 7:	Straighten the left leg and tendu the right leg in back. Allongé both arms in croisé.
Count 8:	Close the right foot back into fifth. Both arms lower to preparatory.

Repeat on the left.

2. Mazurka with pas de basque

Begin in fifth position with the right foot front croisé. Arms in preparatory. Lift the arms through first into second to prepare.

Counts 1 to 2:	Pas de basque right then left en dehors. End with the right foot front in fifth croisé.
Count 3:	Pirouette en dehors to the right from fifth. Finish the pirouette and pose with the right foot back in fourth and the left knee bent in front.
Count 4:	Soutenu turn détourné by pulling the right foot into sous-sus behind the left and turning to the right. End in sous-sus croisé, right foot front.
Repeat.	
Counts 1 to 2:	Balancé right then left in écarté.
Count 3:	Pas de basque en dedans with the right foot, finishing with the left foot back in tendu croisé instead of transferring the weight onto it.
Count 4:	Fouetté in tendu ending with the left foot tendu front croisé. Tombé onto the left foot in preparation for a pirouette en dedans to the left.
Count 5:	Pirouette en dedans to the left. End with the right foot front croisé.
Count 6:	Soutenu turn détourné ending in sous-sus with the left foot front croisé.
Count 7:	Retiré the right foot back to balance.
Count 8:	Hold and come down into fifth plié, left foot front croisé.
Repeat on the left.	

3. Petit allegro with pirouettes

Begin in fifth position with the left foot front croisé. Arms in preparatory. Lift the arms through first into second to prepare.

Count 1:	Glissade en face to the right bringing both arms into first through preparatory.
Count 2:	Pas de chat to the right, opening the left arm second and leaving the right arm in first.
Count &:	Dégagé the right leg à la seconde en face. Allongé both arms.

Counts 3 to 4:	Pas de bourrée de sus (over) ending in fifth plié with the left foot front croisé. Arms breathe down to preparatory with the pas de bourrée.
Counts 5 to 8:	Repeat.

Counts 1 to 2:	Jeté battu right and left leaving arms in preparatory.
Count &:	Dégagé the right leg à la seconde en face. Allongé both arms.
Counts 3 to 4:	Pas de bourrée de sus (over) ending in fifth plié with the left foot front croisé.
Counts 5 &:	Soutenu turn détourné ending with the right foot front croisé in fifth plié.
Counts 6 &:	Pirouette en dehors to the right ending with the left foot front croisé, plié in fifth.
Counts 7 &:	Soutenu turn détourné ending with the right foot front croisé in fifth plié.
Counts 8 &:	Straighten and plié in fifth.

Repeat on the left.

4. Medium allegro waltz

Start on the quarter-mark stage left in B plus with the left foot front. Arms breathe open and close from preparatory to prepare.

Counts 1 to 2:	Piqué to first arabesque on the right leg and faille through with the left foot. Arms close into first on the faille.
Counts 3 to 4:	Glissade right. Pas de chat right bringing the arms to fifth, head turns right.
Counts 5 to 8:	Repeat Counts 1 to 4 with the left leg. End with the right foot front in fifth en face.
Counts 1 to 4:	Chassé step temps levé in arabesque (sauté arabesque) right and then left, traveling downstage right. Arms close to first on each chassé. Open the right arm to second on the first temps levé and then the left arm on the second temps levé.
Counts 5 to 8:	Run clockwise in a circular pattern toward the upstage left quarter-mark.
Counts 1 to 12:	Twelve piqué turns to the right, completing a full circle.
Counts 13 to 16:	Chaîné turns right, traveling downstage right. Pose of your choice.

Repeat on the left.

5. Grand allegro

This exercise travels across the floor from corner to corner. Begin in fifth position with the right foot front croisé in the upstage left corner. Arms in preparatory. Arms breathe open and close to prepare.

Counts 1 to 2:	Sissonne faille. Arms to first. Assemblé battu. Arms open to écarté allongé.
Counts 3 to 4:	Repeat.
Counts & 5:	Soutenu turn détourné turning left. Arms close to first. Développé the left leg devant croisé on Count 5. Arms open to croisé.
Count 6:	Hold.
Counts & 7 &:	Run left, right, left toward the downstage right corner. Arms open second and port de bras through preparatory to first.
Counts 8 &:	Grand jeté développé right, run left. Arms in first arabesque.
Counts 1 & 2 &:	Grand jeté développé right and run left twice more. Arms remain in first arabesque throughout the grand jetés.
Count 3:	Piqué arabesque on the right leg in first arabesque effacé.
Count 4:	Run left, right, left, turning the body to face the upstage left corner. Arms open to second.
Count 5:	Grand jeté entrelacé (tour jeté) pushing off the left foot. Arms port de bras into fifth. Land on the right foot effacé. Place the left foot down in fourth. Arms open to second.
Count 6:	Hold the effacé pose.
Counts & 7 &:	Three emboîté jumps to attitude devant traveling downstage right, landing on the left, right, left.
Count 8:	Precipité, grand jeté développé (saut de chat). Arms port de bras into fifth.

Repeat on the left.

Intermediate Level Pointe Work

1. Waltz with turns

This exercise travels across the floor from corner to corner. Begin in the upstage left corner in B plus with the left foot front croisé. Arms in preparatory. Lift the arms through first into second to prepare.

Counts 1 to 2:	Tombé pas de bourrée. Finish in a fourth position croisé preparation for pirouette, left foot front.
Counts 3 to 4:	Pirouette en dehors to the right. Finish croisé in a plié on the left leg, right leg in attitude.
Counts 5 to 6:	Hold attitude croisé in plié. Arms in croisé.
Count 7:	Piqué into first arabesque on the right foot.
Count 8:	Tombé back onto the left foot to balancé left en face. Right arm lifts to fifth. Head to the left.
Count &:	Tombé onto the right foot toward the downstage right corner.
Counts 1 to 2:	Piqué fouetté onto the left foot. Arms port de bras through fifth. End in first arabesque plié facing left.
Counts 3 to 4:	Piqué fouetté onto the right foot. Arms port de bras through fifth. End in first arabesque facing right.
Counts 5 to 8:	Step under with the left foot and piqué right into chaîné turns traveling to the downstage right corner. Pose of your choice.

2. Relevés, développés, and pirouettes

Begin in fifth position with the right foot front croisé. Arms in preparatory. Arms breathe open and close to prepare. This exercise is excellent for pointe work.

Counts 1 to 2:	Spring onto the left foot and développé the right foot croisé devant. Arms to croisé. Close fifth plié.
Counts 3 to 4:	Repeat.
Count 5:	Chassé en avant into a relevé on the right leg in third arabesque.
Count 6:	Hold.
Counts 7 to 8:	Close the left leg back into plié and soutenu turn détourné toward the left foot. Plié fifth croisé on Count 8 with the left foot front.

Counts 1 to 2:	Spring onto the right foot and développé the left leg second, turning front to face en face. Close fifth plié back.
Counts 3 to 4:	Repeat with the right leg développé to second and closing back.
Counts 5 to 6:	Passé the left foot back through retiré into plié fifth.
Counts 7 to 8:	Two quick passés to the back with the right and then the left foot. End in fifth with the right foot front plié.

Repeat the last eight counts starting with the right foot développé to second. End in fifth with the left foot front plié.

Counts 1 to 2:	Tombé pas de bourrée left, ending fifth plié with the right foot front.
Counts 3 to 4:	Tombé pas de bourrée right, ending fourth plié with the left foot front in croisé.
Counts 5 to 6:	Pirouette en dehors to the right.
Counts 7 to 8:	Temps lié back onto the right foot and tendu the left foot devant in croisé. Close the left foot fifth devant.

Repeat on the left.

Intermediate/Advanced Level Barre Work

1. Dégagés

Start in fifth position right foot front, left side to the barre. Arms in preparatory. Lift the arms through first into second and take the barre with the left hand to prepare.

Counts 1 to 2:	Two dégagés with the right leg à la quatrième devant closing each fifth.
Counts & 3:	Coupé the right leg devant and close fifth devant.
Counts & 4:	Dégagé the right leg devant and close fifth devant.
Counts & 5:	Coupé the right leg devant and close fifth devant.
Counts & 6:	Dégagé the right leg à la seconde and close it coupé derrière in plié.

Counts 7 to 8:	Piqué pas de bourrée en dehors en tournant (half turn), turning away from the barre. Finish fifth with the right foot front and the right hand on the barre, left arm in second.
Counts 1 to 4:	Four dégagés with the right (inside) leg à la quatrième devant closing fifth. The last one closes into plié.
Count 5:	Pirouette en dehors a half turn, lifting the right leg to retiré and closing the arms first.
Counts 6 to 7:	Balance on the left leg with right leg in retiré devant, arms in fifth.
Count 8:	Close the right foot back into fifth plié.

Repeat en dedans.

Repeat on the left.

2. Grands battements

Start in fifth position right foot front, left side to the barre. Arms in preparatory. Lift the arms through first into second and take the barre with the left hand to prepare.

Counts 1 to 2:	Grand battement the right leg devant and close fifth devant.
Counts 3 to 4:	Grand battement the right leg devant ending with the right leg in tendu devant.
Counts & 5:	Grand battement the right leg devant ending with the right leg in tendu devant.
Counts & 6:	Grand battement the right leg devant and close fifth plié devant.
Count 7:	Full soutenu turn toward the barre, ending in sous-sus with left foot front and left hand on the barre.
Count 8:	Plié.

Repeat en dedans.

Counts 1 to 4:	Grand battement the right leg à la seconde twice closing back and front.
Counts 5 to 8:	Grand battement à la seconde four times closing back, front, back, front.
Counts 1 to 2:	Grand battement the right leg devant and grand rond de jambe en l'air en dehors, carrying it around to arabesque. Leave the leg open in arabesque.

Counts 3 to 4:	Grand rond de jambe en dedans with the right leg and close fifth plié devant.
Counts 5 to 6:	Changement twice.
Counts 7 to 8:	Soutenu turn toward the barre, half turn to face the left side.

Repeat on the left.

Intermediate/Advanced Level Center Work

1. Petit allegro

Begin in fifth position with the left foot front croisé. Arms in preparatory. Lift the arms through first into second to prepare.

Counts 1 to 4:	Glissade en face, assemblé battu, right and left. Arms go through first to second.
Counts 5 to 6:	Jeté battu closing the right arm first, temps levé.
Counts 7 to 8:	Sauté ballonné with the left leg opening second to 45 degrees and ending coupé front.
Count &:	Tombé front on the left foot and coupé the right foot back.
Counts 1 to 4:	Step sauté ballonné onto the right foot bringing the left foot to 90 degrees second and ending with the left foot coupé derrière. Repeat on the left leg with a step sauté on the left leg and the right leg opening to second and then closing coupé derrière.
Counts 5 to 6:	Piqué pas de bourrée and finish in fifth plié with right foot front croisé.
Counts 7 to 8:	Entrechat quatre two times.

Repeat on the left.

2. Grand allegro waltz

This exercise travels across the floor from corner to corner. Begin in the upstage left corner in B plus with the left foot front croisé. Arms in preparatory. Arms lift through first, and the left arm opens to second as the right arm lifts to fifth to prepare.

Counts 1 to 2:	Temps levé onto the right foot into first arabesque (sauté arabesque on the right leg). The right arm lowers through first into first arabesque. Tombé on the left leg and bring the arms to first. Repeat on the same side on Count 2.
Count 3:	Step onto the right foot to cabriole back with same arms as above.
Count 4:	Run toward the downstage right corner left, right, left.
Count 5:	Grand jeté développé (saut de chat) right in first arabesque.
Counts & 6:	Step left and piqué arabesque onto the right foot in first arabesque.
Counts & 7:	Plié relevé in first arabesque.
Counts & 8:	Chassé step left toward the upstage left corner.
Count 1:	Grand jeté entrelacé (tour jeté), landing on the right foot. Arms lift to fifth.
Counts 2 to 4:	Repeat chassé step entrelacé. Lower the left foot momentarily on Count 4.
Counts & 5:	Step under with the left foot and tombé pas de bourrée right to prepare in fourth with the left foot front croisé, for pirouettes en dehors to the right.
Counts 6 to 7:	Pirouette en dehors to the right. Place the right foot down in fourth back croisé.
Counts & 8:	Precipité, grand jeté développé right. Arms pass through first and lift into fifth.

Repeat on the left.

3. Grand allegro

This exercise travels across the floor from corner to corner. Begin in fifth position with the right foot front effacé, in the upstage left corner. Arms in preparatory. Arms breathe open and close to prepare.

Counts 1 to 2:	Sissonne fermé in first arabesque. Hold the plié on Count 2.
Count 3:	Sissonne fermé in first arabesque again.
Count 4:	Sissonne ouvert, opening the right leg to développé à la seconde while turning to the right to finish facing upstage. Arms lift through fifth, and the left arm opens second.

Count 5:	Pas de bourrée turning right and ending in fifth plié croisé with the right foot front. Arms lower to preparatory.
Counts 6 to 7:	Sissonne faille, assemblé battu over. Arms to first and then allongé to écarté.
Counts & 8:	Tombé pas de bourrée to the right.
Counts & 1:	Run downstage right, left, right. Arms lift to first.
Count 2:	Grand jeté left croisé, landing in attitude. The right arm lifts to fifth, the left arm opens to second into croisé arms.
Counts & 3:	Run downstage right, left, right. Arms close to first.
Count 4:	Assemblé devant brushing left foot devant. Arms open to third arabesque.
Counts 5 to 6:	Tombé pas de bourrée to the left traveling directly left stage.
Count 7:	Glissade to the left brushing the right leg through. Arms to first.
Count 8:	Grand jeté développé left. Arms à deux bras.

Intermediate/Advanced Level Pointe Work

1. Center arabesque exercise

Use a slow waltz tempo. This exercise focuses on rolling down off pointe with control. Begin in B plus with the left foot front croisé. Arms in preparatory. Arms breathe open and close to prepare.

Counts 1 to 2:	Piqué on the right foot to first arabesque effacé. Roll down to plié on the right foot.
Counts 3 to 4:	Pull the left foot through sous-sus to begin a pas de bourrée. Plié in fifth croisé, left foot front.
Counts 5 to 6:	Piqué on the left foot to third arabesque croisé. Roll down to plié on the left foot.
Counts 7 to 8:	Pull the right foot through sous-sus to begin piqué pas de bourrée en tournant to the right, ending in fifth position plié with the right foot front croisé. Arms lower to preparatory.

Counts 1 to 2:	Piqué on the left foot to first arabesque effacé. Roll down to plié on the left foot.
Counts 3 to 4:	Pull the right foot through sous-sus back to begin pas de bourrée. End with tombé over onto the right foot and coupé the left foot back. Right arm closes first, left arm second.
Counts & 5:	Step back onto the left foot, then piqué right and soutenu turn to the right, crossing the left foot front and ending in sous-sus with the right foot front, en face and still on pointe. Arms close to first.
Counts & 6:	Passé the right leg up through retiré and bring both arms to fifth. Close back in fourth croisé to prepare for pirouettes.
Counts 7 to 8:	Pirouette en dehors to the right. End in a pose with the right leg back in fourth.

Repeat on the left. Begin on & with a rond de jambe à terre en dedans of the right leg and stepping on the right leg to be ready to piqué with the left.

2. Pirouettes across the floor

This exercise travels across the floor from corner to corner. Begin in B plus with the left foot front croisé, in the upstage left corner. Arms in preparatory. Arms breathe open and close to prepare.

Counts 1 to 2:	Tombé pas de bourrée to fourth in preparation for pirouettes.
Counts 3 to 4:	Pirouette (double) en dehors. Pose in fourth with the left leg front, left knee bent.

Repeat with triple pirouettes.

Count 1:	Fouetté en dehors in tendu ending with the right leg tendu devant in croisé.
Counts 2 to 3:	Tombé onto the right foot to begin an Italian fouetté, and développé the left leg second, ending with the left leg back in attitude croisé.
Count 4:	Plié on the right leg in third arabesque.
Counts & 5:	Pull the left leg in to pas de bourrée, turning left. End the pas de bourrée with a tombé fourth onto the left foot in croisé to prepare for pirouettes en dedans.
Count 6:	Pirouette en dedans in attitude derrière. Both arms to fifth.

| Count 7: | Plié on the left leg and extend the right leg to arabesque in effacé. Right arm allongé. |
| Count 8: | Pas de bourrée, ending in fifth plié with the right foot front croisé. |

Repeat on the left.

Advanced Level Barre Work

1. Dégagé

Start in fifth position, right foot front, left side to the barre. Arms in preparatory. Lift the arms through first into second and take the barre with the left hand to prepare.

Counts & 1:	Coupé the right foot devant and close it fifth front.
Counts & 2:	Coupé the left foot derrière and close it fifth back.
Counts & 3:	Dégagé devant and close the right foot devant.
Counts & 4:	Coupé the left foot derrière and close it fifth back.
Counts & 5:	Coupé the right foot devant and close it fifth front.
Counts & 6:	Coupé the left foot derrière and close it fifth back.
Counts & 7:	Dégagé the right foot à la seconde and close it back.
Counts & 8:	Coupé the left foot devant and close it fifth front.

Counts & 1:	Coupé the right foot derrière and close it fifth back.
Counts & 2:	Coupé the left foot devant and close it fifth front.
Counts & 3:	Dégagé and close the right foot derrière.
Counts & 4:	Coupé the left foot devant and close it fifth front.
Counts 5 to 7:	Battement cloche back, front, back with the right foot.
Counts & 8:	Piqué the right foot derrière and close fifth back.

Repeat en dedans.

Repeat on the left.

2. Ronds de jambe à terre with port de bras

Start in first position, left side toward the barre. Arms in preparatory. Arms open and close to preparatory and demi-plié. Brush the right leg to tendu devant and carry it à la seconde while straightening the left knee, bringing the arms through first into second and taking the barre with the left hand to prepare.

Counts 1 to 2:	Rond de jambe à terre en dehors two times, ending with the right leg tendu devant in plié on the left leg.
Count &:	Fouetté en dedans leaving the right foot in tendu and remain in plié. The right hand takes the barre, and the right foot (inside) is in tendu back.
Count 3:	Brush the inside right foot devant to 45 degrees through first and relevé.
Count &:	Brush the right foot through first to tendu back again and plié on the left leg.
Count 4:	Fouetté en dehors ending with the right foot in tendu devant while remaining in plié. The left hand takes the barre.

Repeat en dedans. End with the right leg in tendu arabesque.

Counts 1 to 2:	Two ronds de jambe à terre en dehors with the right leg.
Count 3:	Rond de jambe jeté with the right leg en dehors.
Count 4:	Brush the right leg through first to tendu devant.
Counts 5 to 7:	Repeat Counts 1 to 3 above en dedans.
Count 8:	Close the right foot fifth in front.
Counts 1 to 4:	Port de bras and cambré forward only in sous-sus. Come up and retiré the right leg devant.
Counts 5 to 8:	Port de bras and cambré back, maintaining the retiré devant with the right leg.
Counts 1 to 2:	Passé the right leg back into attitude derrière and bring both arms to fifth.
Counts 3 to 6:	Balance in attitude.
Counts 7 to 8:	Allongé the right leg back to arabesque, close it fifth devant in plié bringing both arms to preparatory.

Repeat on the left.

Advanced Level Center Work

1. Petit allegro

Begin in fifth position with the left foot front en face. Arms in preparatory. Arms breathe open and close to prepare.

Count 1:	Assemblé derrière with the right leg. Arms remain in preparatory.
Count 2:	Assemblé battu dessus (over) with the right leg. Arms remain in preparatory.
Count 3:	Glissade left. Arms remain in preparatory.
Count 4:	Assemblé battu dessus (over) with the left leg. Arms remain in preparatory.
Count 5:	Glissade right. Arms remain in preparatory.
Count 6:	Brisé, brushing the right leg forward from the back. Right arm opens to first. Left arm opens second.
Count 7:	Pas de chat right.
Count 8:	Pas de bourrée, ending in fifth plié with the right foot front en face.

Repeat on the left.

2. Petit/medium allegro

Begin in fifth position with the left foot front croisé. Arms in preparatory. Lift the arms through first into second to prepare.

Counts 1 to 2:	Jeté battu right and left en face, closing the right and then the left arm into first.
Counts 3 to 4:	Rock back and forth through coupé onto the back and then front foot.
Counts 5 to 6:	Step back onto the right foot and sauté ballonné with the left foot opening to 90 degrees à la seconde and closing coupé derrière. Arms lift to fifth and open second.
Counts 7 to 8:	Step back onto the left leg, sauté ballonné with the right leg opening effacé devant at 45 degrees, sauté ballonné écarté

derrière at 45 degrees, ending with the right foot in coupé derrière.

Counts & 1:	Step back onto the right foot and then forward onto the left into a cabriole in first arabesque effacé. Arms go through first into first arabesque.
Count 2:	Tombé forward onto the right foot in croisé and coupé the left foot back.
Counts & 3:	Step back onto the left foot and then forward onto the right into a cabriole in first arabesque effacé. Arms go through first into first arabesque.
Counts & 4:	Faille through onto the left foot and pas de chat right, turning en face.
Counts 5 to 6:	Glissade right, assemblé battu over. Arms go through first into second allongé.
Counts 7 to 8:	Entrechat cinq ending with the left foot in coupé derrière. Then assemblé the left leg derrière. Arms breathe down to preparatory.
Repeat on the left.	

3. Grand allegro

This exercise travels across the floor corner to corner from the upstage left corner. Begin facing the upstage left corner in B plus with the left foot front. Arms in preparatory. Arms breathe open and close to preparatory on Counts 5 to 6. On Count 7, piqué arabesque onto the right foot, facing the upstage left corner. Run left, right, left, turning left toward the downstage right corner on Count 8 to prepare.

Count 1:	Grand jeté entrelacé (tour jeté) pushing off the left foot. Finish facing the upstage left corner with arms in second.
Count 2:	Run left, right, left, turning left toward the downstage right corner. Arms close first.
Count 3:	Cabriole devant effacé, brushing the right leg devant to 90 degrees. Arms effacé.
Counts & 4:	Run right, left. Arms port de bras through second and preparatory, then lift to first.
Count 5:	Grand jeté développé with right leg. Arms in first arabesque.

Counts & 6:	Run left, right, left. Arms port de bras through second and preparatory, then lift to first.
Count 7:	Piqué to first arabesque onto the right leg effacé.
Count 8:	Run left, right, left, turning toward the upstage left corner. Arms close to first.
Count 1:	Grand fouetté sauté, brushing the right leg devant. Arms lift to fifth and open second.
Count 2:	Run right, left, right, turning toward the upstage left corner. Arms close to first.
Count 3:	Assemblé battu en tournant, brushing the left leg and turning one and a half times to the right. Arms lift to fifth. End in fifth position plié croisé, left foot front.
Count 4:	Sissonne changé ouvert, turning a three-quarter turn to the right into croisé on the right leg, left leg attitude derrière. Arms in croisé.
Counts & 5:	Assemblé battu, beating the left leg back, front, and closing the left leg front in plié on &. On Count 5, soutenu turn détourné, turning to the right and ending in sous-sus with the right foot front croisé.
Counts 6 to 7:	Tombé pas de bourrée traveling to the right.
Counts & 8:	Glissade, grand jeté développé (saut de chat). Arms to fifth.

Repeat on the left.

Chapter 7

The Virtual Ballet Classroom

I share this story for the sake of demonstrating the capacity of the dance world to grow and adapt. And I share my virtual teaching suggestions because virtual education is here to stay.

In 2020, the COVID-19 pandemic created an imperative to reinvent how we teach, practice, stage performances, and generally run our performing arts businesses. Virtual dance classes became the industry standard during the pandemic and have remained an accepted mode of teaching dance, as there are ongoing reasons to teach and attend classes virtually. Snow days, travel impediments, scheduling convenience—these are all reasons a dancer may choose to attend class virtually. Or, from the teacher's perspective, a school may decide to host a master class with a well-known instructor who lives thousands of miles away. A virtual class makes it possible for students to experience the wisdom of these teachers no matter where they are in the world.

As the first school and business shutdowns occurred in the United States during the pandemic, dance academies had to make hard choices regarding how to operate without being permitted to hold classes on-site. I saw this play out in several ways. A few schools did nothing at all and closed up shop, leaving their students without classes and looking for alternatives. Some schools offered no regular schedule of classes but did schedule weekly or semiweekly master and guest classes through virtual meeting platforms.

I taught in a couple of different schools and had very different experiences with each. One school was caught off guard by the pandemic and struggled with how best to adapt. Administrators moved regularly scheduled, in-person classes to all-virtual meeting platforms but otherwise showed little leadership beyond transporting students into a new reality and asking them to carry on for the sake of their dancing goals. Students who remained at these schools took their classes virtually from home but often did so without enthusiasm and had difficulty developing skills, grit, and a sense of pride in accomplishing new things. Within the virtual classroom, I aimed to encourage and fortify the hearts and minds of my students, but the administration offered scant guidance in this area.

I was also connected with a school that accepted the challenge and adopted a new way of teaching with dedication and a determination to keep its students committed to the school and their training. In addition to making the technical transition to virtual classes, this school communicated immediately and regularly with its students, providing information about the new teaching methods and offering supportive educational materials on how to build the best home-based class experience. Instructors and administrators teamed up with students and their families, asking them to trust that the school would not let them down in offering the best options for quality education. Students were challenged—not only by me but also through regular assurance and incentives from the school—to remain resilient and see the pandemic through, to become stronger in the face of the unexpected. At this school, we did more than survive; we found ourselves with devoted students and accomplished dancers who owned a new confidence in their abilities to do hard things and emerge as more robust humans and skilled dancers on the other side.

My first week teaching in a virtual ballet classroom was nerve-racking. I'd created a story in my head that the technology involved in virtual training was too complicated for me and I wouldn't be able to figure it out. I was wrong about that and proved myself wrong by doing it anyway. I learned how to hold virtual meetings and to work with the required technology. I researched online, watched instructive videos, and asked the advice of colleagues. With time, I developed my own methods that, I'm happy to report, seemed to work. In the sections that follow, I offer advice derived from this personal experience.

The At-Home Class Space

If you're teaching from home—or from any space other than a dance studio—you'll want to use a room where you have as much space as possible to move around and position your camera. The camera ought to be far enough away to allow your students to observe your entire body, head to toe. Be prepared to adjust the camera angle at times to focus the view on your feet or some other body part if you need to demonstrate something specific. Ensure that there is enough lighting in your room for students to observe your movement without struggle and that there are no overwhelming glares at certain times of the day, which could flood out your students' screen vision.

Your flooring is essential as well. Teaching ballet and jumping on wood or any other hard surface at home can cause pain to the ankles, knees, and back. Teaching on a carpet is also problematic and can cause twisting in the ankle or knee. You may not have any other alternative, but it's valuable to consider the options within your home. It may be worth it to invest in a portable Marley floor or a hard foam gym mat. You will also need a barre. If you can purchase a portable barre, that's helpful. You can also use the back of a sturdy chair, a table, or a counter or ledge. Keep distractions to a minimum. Barking dogs and crying children are realities of life that can't be dismissed, but it's crucial to reduce such interruptions as much as possible while you're teaching.

Virtual Class Structure and Content

What can you actually do? How much can you cover in a virtual ballet class? While you do need to alter the design of the class, you should be able to cover a considerable amount of the classical vocabulary. To start, you need to consider the spaces in which both you and your students are dancing. Some will have little floor space and will be unable to travel. Others may be on carpeting or a very hard floor and unable to jump well or work on pointe. (Although we would prefer they invest in a portable dance floor, expecting this is unrealistic.) Some dancers may have only a flimsy support as a barre. Overall, our goal and responsibility as teachers is to adapt our class and offer modifications to students as necessary.

At-home time is an excellent opportunity to focus on conditioning exercises, which often require only a floor. (When stretching at home, students should not use their chairs as barres, because they're not supportive enough to be safe.) What technical, strength, or flexibility issues have you wanted to address in your students: turnout, foot articulation, supporting-side strength? You can seize this virtual classroom time to focus on all the above. *(For a catalog of conditioning exercises, see Chapter 4.)*

Barre work at home can be similar to that in a typical ballet class, but center work allows for less movement and requires adjustments. If your dancers can't turn on their home floors, offer the modification of simply holding a balance on relevé. If they can't jump, have them do relevés or passés. In the center, you should be able to accomplish tendus, dégagés, adagio, pirouettes, and jumps in place (with modifications as necessary). Traveling across the floor is the biggest hurdle. Many students will have only a few feet of space. So, you'll need to get creative. Create a waltz combination that hardly travels but turns to face different directions. Include only one or two piqué turns in your exercises. To replace grand allegro combinations, give your students exercises to build stamina and power. Strength-building jumps that dancers can do at home without much traveling include multiple temps levés on each foot, grand sissonne ouvert, assemblé, and tours en l'air. Repetition of any of these lesser-traveling jumps will build stamina in addition to strength.

Fully Virtual vs. Hybrid Teaching

You may find yourself teaching a combination of students: those who are in the studio with you in person, and those who are taking the class virtually from their own space. Students attending class virtually will have both space and physical restrictions and may also have audio and visual limitations regarding what they're able to see and do. The virtual student in a hybrid class may be considered a follow-along student, meaning they are there to follow the class and do the exercises at home, but should not expect to have the benefit of receiving corrections or having combinations adapted to their space. Many schools providing hybrid classes offer a discount to students who choose to attend virtually. Each classroom situation is different. Some suggestions I offer are most helpful in the entirely virtual environment while others work best in hybrid circumstances. Pick and choose as best suits your needs.

Helpful Hints for Virtual Teaching

Finally, in no particular order, here are some additional ideas for making your virtual classrooms run smoothly:

1. Have dancers on mute during most of the class except during private lessons. Ask dancers to un-mute themselves if they have a question and then mute themselves again after it is answered.

2. Do not allow students to turn off their cameras at any time during the class.

3. Make sure the lighting in the space where you are teaching is bright enough to see your arms when they're lifted en haut and all the way down to your feet.

4. When you're teaching and demonstrating an exercise, angle the camera so your students can see your entire body if possible. You will need to change the camera angle during class if it does not capture your whole body adequately.

5. If you are demonstrating movement as the dancers do it at home, you may choose to do it with your back to the camera, so they see you doing it in the same directions as themselves.

6. Once an exercise begins, if you're not needed to demonstrate, move close to the screen to watch your students and offer corrections. Even at home, you should be moving from place to place.

7. If possible, use a source of music separate from your computer (or whatever you're using for your virtual meeting platform), and use a Bluetooth or other speaker for music output. Keep the speaker close to the device you're using to broadcast, but be careful to keep your music source at enough distance from the speaker to prevent painful audio feedback.

8. Be aware of the time lag between what you hear and what your virtual students hear in their own spaces. It's often only a fraction of a second, but it's real and can make your students appear to be off the music.

9. If you need to teach choreography virtually, this is the time to simplify. Although we love the complexity of a canon or moving the dancers around the space in compelling patterns, this is not the time to do so unless you are working with advanced or professional dancers. Keep dancers in simple lines, dancing chiefly in unison.

10. If your students need to remember a piece of choreography, make a video—or have one of the students make a video—and email it to everyone to help their memories.

Chapter 8

Words of Wisdom

If I had a mere fifteen minutes in a room with a group of students who wanted to be ballet dancers and I knew I would never see them again, here are the four things I would impart—points that make up the core of my philosophy and which bear repeating:

1. Build your foundation of technique, alignment, and musicality first. Learn the correct way to use your muscles for alignment and turnout. You will have a much stronger base to stand on, and your body will be able to endure the rigors of classical training for much longer. Allow the music to guide your movement. Later, you can build upon this technical and musical foundation, learn all the fancy steps, and adapt to anything.

2. Trust your teachers. Any lack of trust or second-guessing of the professionals working to help you creates an invisible wall between you and them. You will absorb less of their enthusiasm and information, making it harder for you to learn.

3. Remember that ballet is a performance art. We present it to an audience. Technical soundness is the foundation, but you should use classroom and rehearsal time to work on performance qualities as well. Hone your capacity to make your presence felt all the way to the back of a theater by sending energy out from your eyes and collarbone through the walls of the classroom. Dance to tell a story. It can be a deep and complicated story

of love lost or an elegant, simple interpretation of something striking you hear in the music. Ballet should *always* illustrate the music.

4. If dance is your passion, go after it with persistence and *dream big*. Know your *why* and keep that idea with you through all the long classes and rehearsals. Each of those long classes is a gift to yourself in the future because it brings you one step closer to living your dream. Pursue your goals doggedly while being honest about your weaknesses so you can turn them into strengths. Know your superpowers as a dancer so that you can emphasize them. Use it all to make your goals a reality. Go into the world and do!

These are my truisms. How did I come to this approach? Partly through my own training along with a good amount of trial and error as a teacher but also in part by observing, hearing, and reading the words of outstanding teachers over the years. Excellent teachers inspire me to be a better teacher and have many times taught me new methods for approaching dance education. So, when I set out to write this book, I figured, why not share other instructors' invaluable wisdom here?

I reached out to professional dancers, many of whom have been my students, and asked them to choose the teacher who'd been most influential in their training and eventual career. I then reached out to those teachers who generously shared their sage advice, and I leave it with you here.

"Answers unfold slowly with time, reflection, and practice."

"I think the biggest idea is that dance training is a process. There are no quick fixes or shortcuts involved. Answers unfold slowly with time, reflection, and practice. And the benefits of training translate so easily into other aspects of life. From training, we learn that frustration doesn't always last forever, that 'aha!' moments do happen, and that growth can be measurable."

Laura Martin is a member of the Ballet Department faculty at the University of North Carolina School of the Arts.

Laura Martin was chosen by Lyssa Wopat, an artist with the Georgia Ballet.

"Know how ballet works best for the individual body."

"I'm a master teacher in Revolutionary Principles of Movement. When it comes to technique, I feel that the dancer needs to know how ballet works best for the individual body. Artistically (and technically), choose other, more advanced dancers as role models you can learn from. And discover your own superpowers! We all have them. Then work harder on your deficiencies."

Wes Chapman, an internationally renowned master teacher, was formerly ballet master at American Ballet Theatre and artistic director of the ABT Studio Company

Wes Chapman was chosen by April Giangeruso, a member of the corps de ballet at American Ballet Theatre.

"Study your body like a scientist."

"Study your body like a scientist. The more you know about the inner workings of your instrument (how it functions to keep you alive and thriving, its structural limitations and possibilities), the more likely you will be to develop a healthy, sophisticated, and sustainable practice for a lifelong career in dance. Through practice in experiential anatomy, I find students are also able to develop a deep connection to the relationship between kinesthetic experience and environmental communication. Whether they're studying ballet, contemporary dance, or any other performative form, I am riveted by performers who are able to make visible their inner landscape."

Stephanie Nugent is artistic director of Nugent Dance and a member of the dance faculty at Indiana University Bloomington's Department of Theatre, Drama, and Contemporary Dance.

Stephanie Nugent was chosen by Susie Wopat a company member
with Company Danzante.

"Demand a lot of yourself."

"To be very good at something, you have to demand a lot of yourself. A dancer who wants to be the best will listen to every correction the teacher gives, no matter whom it's directed toward, and apply that correction to themselves. By an inch or a mile, keep moving forward."

Susan Joines teaches at Centre Pointe Performing Arts in White Marsh, Maryland, which she previously founded as Dancemoves Studio of Dance.

Susan Joines was chosen by Kelly Sneddon, a former dancer at Complexions Contemporary Ballet.

"Your body has the ability to correct itself."

"Your body is not a puppet for your brain. Bodies learn in layers and, especially with complex movement, by trial and error. This means that errors are actually essential to the learning process. Stay mentally neutral in class and notice what's going well in addition to what's going wrong, without judgment or emotion. Trust and listen and respond to your unique body and respect that it learns differently from your head. Your body has the ability to correct itself on balance, turns, speed of motion, and many other aspects of dance if you just give it the space and time and repetitions it needs."

Shari Vegso is the director of Susquehanna Dance Center and the artistic director of Cobalt Dance Company, both in Mountville, Pennsylvania.

Shari Vegso was chosen by Emily Bailey, a trainee with Nashville Ballet.

"You can enrich the lives of others."

"You have been given the gift of life. To find success in life as well as in show-biz, think of how you can enrich the lives of others and simply make yourself desirable."

**Jo Rowan is the director and founder of the American Spirit Dance Company
and chair of the Ann Lacy School of American Dance and Entertainment at Oklahoma City University,
where she founded the dance program.**

Jo Rowan was chosen by Kerry Bruso, a full-time dancer with
Walt Disney World in Orlando, Florida.

"Trust the process."

"Being an artist is equally as important as being a technician. Young students are often so enamored by large tricks and technical difficulty that they forget that ballet is an art form. Artistic quality is the icing on the cake needed to become a true professional.

"Basics are everything. If you want to become advanced, be a good beginner. You can't go straight from A to Z. The only way to truly improve is the old-fashioned way of hard work, trust, determination, and perseverance! Trust the process; there are no shortcuts to becoming a great dancer."

Ashley Canterna Hardy owns and directs Artistic Movement Academy of Dance in Glen Burnie, MD, as well as teaching and choreographing throughout the Maryland and Washington DC area.

Ashley Canterna Hardy was chosen by Derek Dunn, a Youth America Grand Prix gold medalist and principal dancer with the Boston Ballet.

"Be brave."

"The single greatest piece of wisdom [Mr. Balanchine] passed on was to be brave, to be generous in effort, not to hold back, not to be merely safe, not to save energy when one can always summon more will to transcend limits. Transcending one's perceived limits takes one to previously unimagined heights of accomplishment and expression, a journey one can only discover by truly committing to get beyond fatigue and self-doubt."

Daniel Duell, Ballet Chicago Artistic Director, chose George Balanchine and shares his inspirational words. As a dancer with the New York City Ballet from 1972–1987, Mr. Duell was taught and coached daily by George Balanchine.

George Balanchine is considered to be the father of American ballet.
He co-founded the New York City Ballet and remained its artistic director
for more than thirty-five years.

Ballet's Lessons Beyond the Classroom

Classical ballet training routinely creates ballet dancers. But most people who pursue classical training do not become professionals. This isn't a bad thing, however. In fact, it's perfectly wonderful because ballet training has intrinsic value. It instills qualities and skills in students that can lead to many other careers.

Serious ballet training inspires discipline, physical coordination and health, drive, grit, and the ability to set long-term goals. It develops students' focus and teaches them to learn new concepts quickly, which is excellent for cultivating memory. Trained dancers learn how to overcome obstacles. They master the skills of working well in groups of all types of people and being responsible for the whole. The ballet class also gives many of its participants a sanctuary. Yes, that sanctuary is filled with hard work, sweat, and constant battles with our bodies and minds, but it is also filled with love, beauty, and devotion.

Getting back to those skills though—what is gained in ballet training can lend itself to a multitude of other careers. Any career requiring diligence, attention to detail, and long-term goal setting is benefited by ballet training. Physical therapists and fitness instructors benefit from all the body-work knowledge. Photographers who've trained in ballet use their knowledge of line, pattern, and timing to develop an aesthetic or capture bodies in motion. Ballet-trained writers draw on their musicality to inform the rhythms of their prose. Even careers that may appear unrelated to dance are enhanced by the rigors and discipline of ballet training. For example, I spent years as a medical assistant. The doctor for whom I worked was routinely impressed by my work ethic, the speed with which I memorized new information, and my consistently high level of performance. I told him what I knew to be true: "Hire another ballet dancer, and you will continue to find a superior level of ability and accomplishment."

So perhaps this book's readers and their students will go on to magnificent ballet careers. Or maybe they'll blossom in life outside the world of ballet, thanks to the lessons their dance training has taught them. Either way, I hope that with this book, I've built a bridge to carry ballet teachers, dancers, and ballet lovers to a place of understanding—an understanding of how to teach and dance the technique, of how to build a better dancer, and of how to be a dancer, in the classroom and out in the world.

Acknowledgments

As I complete this project, I realize I did not do it alone. I had the help of so many people. I hope I have thanked them all here. I know, however, I have missed some people who deserve my public gratitude. Please know any unmentioned names go unmentioned because of my lack of memory and not because of a lack of appreciation.

The true beginnings of this book arise from the hours I spent in ballet class with my own ballet teachers. Some of these teachers lit the spark that became the dancing fire in my heart. Some believed in me so much that I learned to believe in myself. Others shared their knowledge with masterful communication. A few pushed me to the highest standards: standards I had not realized I wasn't reaching without their push. And there were teachers who taught me by example how to manage a classroom and set goals for my students. Today, I am still infused with the training experiences from my past. I wish I could remember the name of every teacher I was ever graced to have standing in front of me in a ballet class. Sadly, my memory is not that excellent. What I can do is share the names of the teachers who had the most profound impact on my dancing and my current teaching. I am bound in gratitude to the following teachers. They all played a role in my becoming: Harriet Eisner, Wally Saunders, Thomas Hanner, Wendy Robinson, Petrus Bosman, Christine Henessy, David Keener, Christine Vilardo, Stephanie FarenWald Sands, Melinda Howe, Dennis Price, and Nancy Wanich Romita.

As an adult and experienced teacher, I had considered and wanted to write a book for about five years before I actually put pen to paper—or fingers to keyboard. I have Brooke Castillo to thank for teaching me how to set and meet a goal.

Along the way, there were friends and family who encouraged me to do this thing. They reassured me that I had something valuable to say. My deep thanks to my sister, Melissa Engerman; my mom, Karan Engerman; my dad, Jay Engerman; and my in-laws, Janie and Jim Turner. And to all of these friend gems as well: Anne O'Brien, Deb Henry, Nicolle Cannapp, Adrian Brown, Melissa Feliciano, Susan Joines, Amy Martin Williams, Adrienne Canterna, Ashley Canterna Hardy, Michelle Rae Owczarzak, my Bryn Mawr School Class of '86 friends, Becca Friedman, Pete Commander, Barclay Gibbs, Danielle Forgione, Krista Ramirez, and Jamie Anderson.

Then there were the friends who went a step beyond encouraging words, and read sections of my writing, offering honest feedback. For your time, effort, and honesty, I thank you, Statia Smith, Grant Robinson, and Karyn Edison. I am grateful for the same time and input from Tamian Wood and Rosalie Mastaler who provided expert advice without knowing me, simply in an act to pay it forward.

The photos in this book were taken during the COVID-19 pandemic. Participants had to tolerate multiple schedule changes, social distancing, and mask-wearing for long days of shooting. Many thanks to the gifted photographer, Scott Serio. And to all of the dancers who generously shared their time and talents: Adrienne Canterna, Kelly Sneddon, Christine Blackshaw, Belle Brown, Natalie Fitch, Jada Simms, Rilee Anderson, Madison Zinkand, Liz Devanney, Emily Bailey, and Magnolia Williams.

I want to recognize Tia Colborne as well. As a dance professional and an editor/writer, she graced me with her support and knowledge.

Birgitte Necessary is an experienced dancer and writer who offered advice and support. I am grateful the Universe brought us together.

I had a new angel in my corner during this venture, Susan Ashley, offering unwavering support and advice.

In the middle of the book-writing process, I experienced my own health crisis and needed additional photos urgently. Thank you to the brilliant photographer Ashley Smith who stepped in on short notice to photograph me teaching classes. You can see her classroom photos in the book. The photo of me on the back cover is also a product of Ashley's company, Wide-Eyed Studios.

Thank you to Charm City Ballet and Susquehanna Dance Center for the use of their beautiful studio space.

I want to recognize my copy editor, Carly Catt, and my book designer, Susi Clark, for their expertise and patience. They each answered approximately 7,000 questions from this nervous newbie. With patience. With enthusiasm. Without condescension.

Getting this book to publication involved many challenges, not the least of which was my failing to forgive myself for being human—and all that entails. Sarah Lane opened a door for me by suggesting that I, too, deserve blessings. That grace has kept me moving forward in this project. Thank you, Sarah, from the bottom of my heart.

The last two people are the most important, and I am most indebted to these two people. First, my husband, Dave Turner. My scientist, football-loving (read non-dancer) husband. He never doubted or complained throughout my entire process. He read chapters and offered feedback and generally indulged me in my project-based whims. I love you, Dave.

Lastly, my editor, Jen Balderama. She possesses all of the writing and dance knowledge to have been more help and inspiration than I could have imagined receiving. This project was blessed the day she crossed my path. Jen was able to read my awkward words, understand what I wanted to say but was not saying, and ask me just the right questions needed in order to help me "say what I mean" clearly and authentically. She was often able to word my sentences better than I, all while guarding my precise intention. I am a better writer for knowing Jen.

About the Author

Deborah Engerman trained under Wally Saunders in Pikesville, Maryland, from 1977 to 1979, and with the Baltimore Ballet School (formerly the Maryland Ballet School) under the direction of Wendy Robinson from 1979 to 1985, in the RAD (Royal Academy of Dance) tradition. Her classical studies also included training with Petrus Bosman, David Keener, and Christine Hennessy at National Academy of the Arts and Virginia School of the Arts. While pursuing her Bachelor of Arts in International Policy and Management Studies at Dickinson College from 1986 to 1990, she continued her study of classical ballet with the teachers of Central Pennsylvania Youth Ballet. Her dance training includes Vaganova technique, French methodology, Martha Graham technique, and the Dance Education Program at Towson University. She has staged ballets including The Nutcracker and Swan Lake: Act II.

For more than three decades, dancers under Engerman's tutelage have gone on to earn professional contracts and danced with companies including American Ballet Theatre, Ballet Inc., Boston Ballet, Complexions Contemporary Ballet, Hubbard Street Dance Chicago, Nashville Ballet, Texture Ballet, Universal Ballet, the Vienna Opera Ballet, the Washington Ballet, and on Broadway. She has also coached dancers for numerous international competitions, such as the Prix de Lausanne, the Varna International Ballet Competition, and Youth America Grand Prix. Her student Adrienne Canterna took the Junior Gold Medal at the 1998 Jackson USA International Ballet Competition.

For most of 2010, Engerman toured Europe as ballet mistress for Rock the Ballet, of Sweetbird Productions. Back in the United States, from 2010 to 2020, she was director of the Maryland Classical Dance Academy at Centre Pointe Performing Arts, and simultaneously trained students at Charm City Ballet, Dance Conservatory of Maryland, and Susquehanna Dance Center. Mrs. Engerman continues to contribute to the future of ballet by training dancers throughout Maryland and Pennsylvania. She lives with her husband and two canine companions in South Central Pennsylvania.

Index

Note: Figures are indicated by an italic f following the page number.

C